IN HIS PRESENCE
Visits to 'Abdu'l-Bahá

'ABDU'L-BAHÁ

IN HIS PRESENCE

Visits to 'Abdu'l-Bahá

Memoirs of:
Roy Wilhelm
Stanwood Cobb
Genevieve L. Coy

KALIMÁT PRESS
LOS ANGELES

Copyright © 1989 by Kalimát Press.
All Rights Reserved.
Manufactured in the United States of America.

Knock, and It Shall Be Opened Unto You was originally published as a booklet by the author in 1908. *Memories of 'Abdu'l-Bahá* was published in the July-August 1962 issues of *Bahá'í News*, and as a separate booklet by the author (n.d.). "A Week in 'Abdu'l-Bahá's Home" was first published in *Star of the West*, Vol. 12, Nos. 10–13, in 1921.

Library of Congress Cataloging-in-Publication Data

Wilhelm, Roy.
In his presence.

Contents: Preface by Richard Hollinger—Knock and it shall be opened unto you / by Roy Wilhelm—Memories of 'Abdu'l-Bahá / by Stanwood Cobb—A week in 'Abdu'l-Bahá home / by Genevieve L. Coy.

1. 'Abdu'l-Bahá. 1844–1921. 2. Baha'is—Biography. I. Cobb, Stanwood, b. 1881. II. Coy, Genevieve Lenore, b. 1889. III. Title.

BP393.W55 1989   297'.93'092 [B]   89–11076
ISBN 0-933770-71-5

CONTENTS

Preface vii

Knock, and It Shall Be Opened Unto You
by Roy Wilhelm 3

Memories of 'Abdu'l-Bahá
by Stanwood Cobb 25

A Week in 'Abdu'l-Bahá's Home
by Genevieve L. Coy................. 67

'ABDU'L-BAHÁ

PREFACE

'Abdu'l-Bahá has always held a special place in the hearts of Western Bahá'ís. This is not simply because of His station as the Center of Covenant, which is acknowledged by all Bahá'ís, or even because of His saintly life. The Bahá'í communities in Europe and America came into being during the ministry of 'Abdu'l-Bahá. Large numbers of the early believers had been taught that 'Abdu'l-Bahá was the Return of Christ and had accepted Him as such. Though their understanding of His true station would change, 'Abdu'l-Bahá would remain their Master, the Head of their Faith, and the perfect Example of what it was to be a Bahá'í. For many, He remained the living embodiment of the *numenus*.

'Abdu'l-Bahá effectively adapted His presentation of the Bahá'í Teachings to this new Western audience. He addressed issues that were current and controversial in the West and, at times, He even adopted Western styles of discourse. These early Bahá'ís had little access to the Writings of the Báb and Bahá'u'lláh. For them, the major corpus of their Sacred Scripture consisted of the Tablets (i.e., letters) of 'Abdu'l-Bahá.

In these early days, there were only two avenues of communication with 'Abdu'l-Bahá. The first was through correspondence. American Bahá'ís began writing to 'Abdu'l-Bahá as early as 1894, and He received an almost continuous stream of letters from Bahá'ís in the West from that time on. His replies, the fruits of this correspondence, are collected in such books as *Selections from the Writings of 'Abdu'l-Bahá, Bahá'í World Faith*, and *Tablets of Abdul Baha*.

The second avenue of communication with the Master was meeting Him in person. Before His travels to Europe and America (1911–1913) such meetings were only possible for pilgrims who journeyed to Palestine, where He resided. In the almost quarter century during which this option existed, a significant number of Bahá'ís did travel from the West to the Holy Land. Of course, the majority of Bahá'ís never did. And so, to share their experiences with their fellow believers, the pilgrims often published or circulated manuscripts with descriptions of their trips.

The value of these "pilgrim's notes" to the Bahá'í community has changed over time. Most of them consisted only of transcripts of 'Abdu'l-Bahá's table talks, as they were recorded or remembered by the pilgrims. At the time, these notes provided important insights on issues that were not addressed in the limited Bahá'í Scripture that was published and available.

However, the accuracy of the notes, the quality of the transcription and the translation, was always open to question. Indeed, pilgrims could and did return from Palestine with contradictory reports of 'Abdu'l-Bahá's teachings and instructions. Therefore, the Master instructed that these should not be regarded as binding on the community, unless He had Himself reviewed and corrected the notes. Such approved transcriptions of 'Abdu'l-Bahá's talks, in fact, comprise a significant part of His writings available to us today. *Some Answered Questions* is the most important example.

The value to the Bahá'í community of unapproved transcriptions of 'Abdu'l-Bahá's talks has waned with time. There are, however, other pilgrims' notes which recount experiences with 'Abdu'l-Bahá, with only brief accounts of His conversations. In the early years, these had been common. After 'Abdu'l-Bahá's visit to the West, they were published less often. Presumably, this was because most Bahá'ís had been able to meet 'Abdu'l-Bahá themselves, or to talk directly to others who had. Written accounts of visits to 'Abdu'l-Bahá were naturally less sought after—though anecdotes about the Master, and especially the Master in America, became a vital part of the oral culture of the community. Stories from this period still circulate among Bahá'ís today.

At this point, seventy-five years after His trip to America, there are few persons who remain among us who have had the bounty of meeting 'Abdu'l-Bahá in person. Most Bahá'ís have no experience, therefore, of hearing about such meetings first-hand. So, it seems appropriate now to republish some of the more touching accounts of meetings with the Master. Those collected in this book were chosen almost at random: the notes of Roy Wilhelm, Stanwood Cobb, and Genevieve Coy.

Since these believers visited 'Abdu'l-Bahá at different periods during His ministry, their accounts reflect the changes that were occurring

ROY WILHELM

in the Bahá'í world, and especially in the circumstances of 'Abdu'l-Bahá, during this thirteen-year period (1907–1920). Of course, they also reflect the personalities of the authors.

Roy Wilhelm made a pilgrimage with his mother in April, 1907. 'Abdu'l-Bahá was still a prisoner then, confined by the Ottoman authorities to the prison-city of 'Akká. For this reason, He was unable to accompany the pilgrims everywhere. Because of unpredictable prison conditions, most Western pilgrims were allowed to stay in 'Akká for only a short time. Some of those who came to see 'Abdu'l-Bahá during 1907, were turned away completely; others had their visits cut short. The Wilhelms were able to stay in 'Akká for about a week.

Despite such restrictions, the pilgrimage was spiritually invigorating for Roy Wilhelm. He went on to become one of 'Abdu'l-Bahá's most trusted followers in America. It was on his property in West Englewood, New Jersey, that 'Abdu'l-Bahá arranged for a Unity Feast, in an effort to unite the Bahá'ís of the New York area. This choice demonstrates 'Abdu'l-Bahá's confidence and trust in Roy Wilhelm, that his home would be chosen as a place of unity where antagonistic factions might be safely brought together. For years, all of 'Abdu'l-Bahá's letters to America were sent to Roy Wilhelm, who would then forward them on to their intended recipients. He also handled the Master's financial affairs in this country. Because of his faithfulness and devotion to the Cause, he was appointed (posthumously) a Hand of the Cause in 1951.

Stanwood Cobb tells the story of meeting with 'Abdu'l-Bahá on five different occasions. His first visit took place near the end of January 1909, though he recalls the visit to have been in February. Restrictions on the Master's movements had recently been lifted. However, because He was still closely observed, this new freedom was only used cautiously. Stanwood Cobb had the impression, in fact, that He was still under guard. When he returned to the Holy Land in 1910, he saw the Master moving about more freely.

His last three meetings with 'Abdu'l-Bahá took place in the West: Boston, 1912; Washington, D.C., 1912; and Paris, 1913. He felt that the last meeting was the most important, for his own subjective reasons. We learn as much about Stanwood Cobb in these memoirs as we do about 'Abdu'l-Bahá. And this is the

STANWOOD COBB

great value of his remembrances—we catch a glimpse of the effect the Master could have on the thoughts and feelings of the believers, how He could adapt His message to the specific spiritual needs of one individual. It was Stanwood Cobb's willingness to reveal himself in this way, in various publications, that has earned him the reputation of something of a sage in the American Bahá'í community.

Dr. Genevieve Coy went on pilgrimage in 1920, in the company of three other Bahá'í women. They stayed for one week. Her account is valuable in that it holds more details about the daily aspects of her visit. We note that the spread of the Faith around the world was now reflected in the Master's Household: Khusraw, from Burma; Fujita, from Japan; and Mrs. Hoagg, from America, were serving in the Holy Land. More than thirty pilgrims—from Asia and Europe, as well as the United States—were 'Abdu'l-Bahá's guests, including one from Ashkhabad ('Ishqábád), in Russian Turkestan, where the first Bahá'í Temple had been completed.

Genevieve Coy's pilgrimage had a tremendous influence on her life. Within a few months, at the request of 'Abdu'l-Bahá, she was on her way to Tehran to teach in the Bahá'í School for

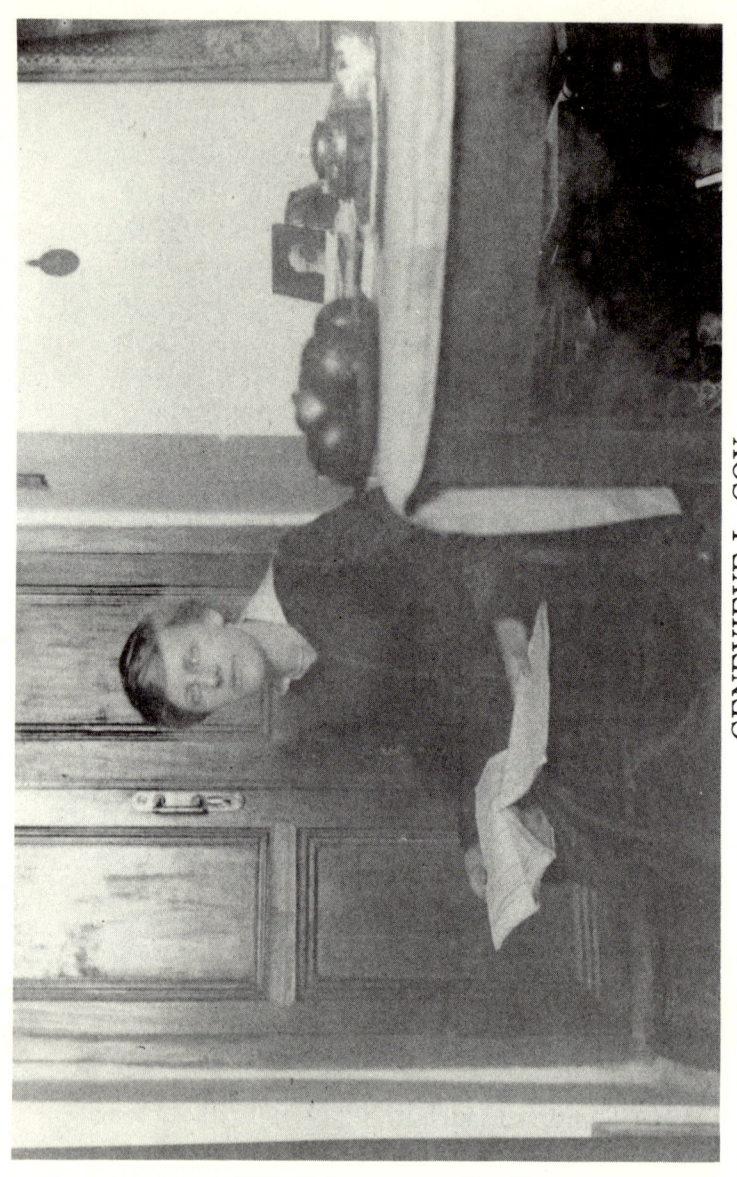

GENEVIEVE L. COY
probably taken in her room in Tehran, Iran.

girls. Returning to America, some years later, she served as a member of the Spiritual Assembly of the Bahá'ís of New York City, as an administrator of the Green Acre Bahá'í School, and in various other capacities until her death in 1963.

A common theme can be found in these, and in most other pilgrim accounts from this period. The correct purpose of Bahá'í pilgrimage is to pray in the Shrines of Bahá'u'lláh and the Báb, the Manifestations of God. But, in reality, the goal of the early pilgrims was to attain the presence of their Master, 'Abdu'l-Bahá. Though He consistently turned their attention to the Holy Shrines, placing the greatest importance on their visits there, it was the presence of 'Abdu'l-Bahá that the pilgrims longed for; meeting with Him transformed their lives; His example caused them to dedicate their remaining years to the service of the Cause.

It is our hope that republishing these accounts will put our own generation of Bahá'ís in touch with a part of our spiritual heritage, deepen our love for 'Abdu'l-Bahá, and confirm our dedication to the Cause of His Father.

—THE EDITORS

9
Knock, and It Shall Be Opened Unto You

1907

by Roy Wilhelm

ROY WILHELM
standing in front of the Bahá'í Temple, Wilmette, Illinois, in later years.

*He that is Greatest Among You
shall be Your Servant.*
                              Matt. 23:11

IN THE PENAL FORTRESS of 'Akká, in Palestine, on the eastern shore of the Mediterranean, the "Tideless Sea," there is a prisoner and an exile. His name is 'Abdu'l-Bahá, which means, the Servant of God. "Behold, my servant, whom I uphold; mine elect, in whom my soul delighteth; I have put my spirit upon him: he shall bring forth judgment to the Gentiles. He shall not cry, nor lift up, nor cause his voice to be heard in the street."*

It was in this Holy Land that Jesus of Nazareth traveled nineteen hundred years ago, preaching and teaching in the streets of the cities the simple Truth of God. It is true that only a few ignorant fishermen were able to comprehend His Message.

That which most impresses the pilgrim to

*Isaiah 42:1–2.

the "Most Great Prison," at 'Akká, is the spirit of sacrifice. Nowhere have I witnessed such love, such perfect harmony. The desire of those in that prison is to serve one another.

In our western liberty it is difficult to realize the bitter antagonism and hatred which exists in the East between the followers of the several great religious systems. For example, a Jew and a Muhammadan would refuse to sit at meat together: a Hindu to draw water from a well of either. Yet, in the house of 'Abdu'l-Bahá we found Christians, Jews, Muhammadans, Zoroastrians, Hindus, blending together as children of the one God, living in perfect love and harmony.

Each of these systems proclaims that it is striving to promote the "Fatherhood of God and the brotherhood of man." To accomplish this end, the Christians have sent out many missionaries into the East, and from the systems of the East have come missionaries into the West. Each has seen the realization of its dream only through the triumph of its own over all the other systems, but during all the centuries none has succeeded in consuming another. It is estimated that the three foremost in point of numbers stand about as follows*: Buddhists, 550,000,000; Christians, 500,000,000; Muhammadans, 350,000,000. Like the Christians, all the others have divided and subdivided into many branches, some of them as antagonistic as the systems themselves.

At the house of 'Abdu'l-Bahá, in 'Akká, we met many of these peoples, but they had lost all trace of the discord and hatred which has been inbred and cultivated for centuries, and now they are as members of one Household. They sacrifice their lives for one another. To what shall we attribute this miracle of unity?

At Port Said, Egypt, a resident Bahá'í came to the steamer with a boat to carry us ashore. After the formalities of the Custom House, we were driven to our hotel, where we remained two days awaiting the arrival of a Russian steamer for Haifa, Syria, the regular steamer being obliged to omit its trip on account of a Sirocco (hot wind and sand storm) which

---

*These populations reflect the situation c. 1908. At present, the numbers would be: Buddhists: 309,626,100; Christians: 1,644,396,500; Muslims: 860,388,300. (*The World Almanac and Book of Facts 1989*)—ED.

came from the desert and visited Port Said the day after our arrival, virtually suspending traffic on both land and water for about twelve hours. The evening of the second day, four of our American friends returning from 'Akká arrived in Port Said, and we had a most interesting meeting with the resident believers. We had heard much of the love and kindness shown by the Oriental brothers to the pilgrims from the West—after our visit to Port Said we understood.

The following evening, April 20th, we sailed on the Russian ship for Haifa. It was still quite rough as a result of the Sirocco. The next morning at eight-thirty we reached Jaffa, the port of Jerusalem, where the unloading of cargo caused a delay. At one o'clock, we left for Haifa and the little vessel was pushed to its fullest capacity in the hope that it might make port before sunset, which would enable the passengers to land. Fortunately, we arrived just in time, and at six-thirty dropped anchor a mile from shore. Owing to the shallowness of the water, passengers are landed in small boats, and this is easy only under the most favorable weather conditions. Although the storm had subsided, there was still some sea running, which made the landing difficult, particularly as it was dark when we reached shore. We were not delayed by the inspection of our baggage and so immediately took a carriage to the Hotel Carmel, which we reached after ten minutes drive.

Our friend at Port Said had given us letters to two merchants in Haifa, but the messenger we dispatched to them returned with the information that both had gone to 'Akká. We had the address of another believer, whose son we knew in this country, and we then sent to him, but it was so late that he did not receive our message until the following morning. He came quite early to the hotel, and his warm welcome made us feel that close relationship into which this Revelation brings all people.

In the afternoon, we went to his home and later visited the Tomb of the Báb,* which is about a mile above Haifa on Mt. Carmel and which overlooks the city and the bay. The Tomb faces 'Akká, which place one can plainly see on a clear day.

I preceded the others a half hour in order to

---

*Now known to Bahá'ís as the Shrine of the Báb.—ED.

make some photographs before the sun was too low. Upon reaching the Tomb I found only one room open and within were several Persians sitting about a table. They did not understand English, but by tapping my camera and making signs I made my wishes known and received permission to take some pictures.

I saw upon the finger of one of them, a venerable man with flowing white beard, a ring such as is worn by many of the believers.* As he was close to me, I whispered in his ear in Arabic the universal Bahá'í greeting†; he immediately cried it aloud, and as he grasped me in his arms and kissed me on both cheeks, the tears came into his eyes. Then they all crowded round, pressing my hands, and I knew that I was among friends. In the meeting of the West with the East is fulfilled the prophecies of the Books.

The following morning, our friend received permission for us to proceed to 'Akká, and we engaged a high-bodied carriage for the drive of ten miles, as two streams had to be forded.

*The symbol engraved on the Bahá'í ringstone is:
—Ed.

†Alláh-u Abhá! (God is most glorious!)—Ed.

THE "ROAD" TO 'AKKÁ.
The early pilgrims traveled along the beach from Haifa to 'Akká.

The smooth hard sand at the edge of the Mediterranean is the road, and as we drove along, the waves would frequently wash up against the horses' feet. The little horses knew that the sand was hardest at the water's edge, and they followed the waves as they washed up and receded, traveling in scallops, as it were. It is a low sandy coast, and the outline is broken only by an occasional clump of date palms and tall cactus plants. We passed here and there an Arab on horseback, usually a long rifle pointing above his shoulder; also a number of natives with their flowing garments girded up into their belts to give greater freedom and to offer less resistance to the wind, which at times blew with considerable force. Above the water line the sand seemed to be constantly shifting into irregular mounds, some of them as much as fifteen or twenty feet in height.

It was after two o'clock when we entered the gate of the prison city, and we were rapidly driven through narrow winding streets, the driver cracking his long whip to warn people at the turnings, and in about five minutes we stopped at a house the entrance to which was an arch having a heavy swinging door. The word "Welcome" greeted our ears, our baggage was removed from the carriage, and we were assisted to the ground and conducted through the entrance so quickly that we did not at once realize we had reached the "Most Great Prison," the end of our seven thousand miles' journey. We passed through a courtyard and up a long flight of stone steps into an upper court from which we were ushered through a dining room into a large square room facing the Mediterranean and overlooking the three crumbling walls that remain of the once strong fortification. Here the welcome was repeated, and we now realized that we were the guests of 'Abdu'l-Bahá. The young man who had been our escort, after inquiring if we were well and if we had had a pleasant journey, informed us that this would be our room and said he would leave us that we might rest.

In about an hour the young man returned with the announcement: "The Master is coming."

As 'Abdu'l-Bahá crossed the threshold He uttered the words, "Welcome! Welcome!" He then led us to a divan which extended the full length of the room, and bade us be seated beside Him. Taking my mother's hand in His

THE CITY OF 'AKKÁ

own and putting His arm around me, He spoke in Persian, addressing us through an interpreter, repeating the greeting, "Welcome! Very Welcome! I have been waiting long for your coming. It is with God's help that you have reached 'Akká. Many leave their homes to come to 'Akká but do not arrive. This is a good day; this a good season of the year because it is Spring. The Cause of God is like a tree—its fruit is love. How are the believers?"

We answered: "They are well and are becoming more united."

He then said: "This news is the cause of my happiness, for the more they are united the more they will receive God's confirmation. They must love one another. Each must devote and sacrifice himself and what he has for the other. I, myself, sacrifice my life for all. You represent all the American believers. In you I see all the American believers. Your faces are shining. I have been waiting long for your coming. Thank God that you came."

We replied: "We do thank God and hope to become worthy."

And He answered: "You will become more worthy."

We remained in 'Akká six days, and each

day other pilgrims came to our room. Some of them related incidents of their personal experience with Bahá'u'lláh, and concerning the early days of the Revelation. One, a Persian, told us he had been striving to come to 'Akká for twenty-two years, but had been deterred by the threats of his brother to announce that he was a Bahá'í.* He said that his only thought was for his wife and children, but that the yearning to meet 'Abdu'l-Bahá had finally become so strong that he could no longer defer making the pilgrimage. To our inquiry as to what he thought might result upon his return, he replied, "That remains with God."

Our room fronted upon a little garden in which was a fountain, and nearby a tent in which 'Abdu'l-Bahá receives many of those who come to see Him. So intense are the hatreds between the followers of the different religious systems that it is unusual for a man to be well spoken of outside his own system, but

---

*Four years ago, one hundred and seventy Bahá'ís were martyred in his city during a period of four days. —R.W.

This refers to the persecution of the Bahá'ís of Yazd in 1903.—Ed.

THE HOUSE OF 'ABBÚD
where 'Abdu'l-Bahá was imprisoned in 'Akká.

'Abdu'l-Bahá is regarded by all classes as a man of such wisdom and justice that it is to Him that they come for explanations of their religious Books, for the adjustment of their business quarrels, and even for the settlement of family difficulties. The inquirer will be told that 'Abbás Effendi ('Abdu'l-Bahá) makes no distinction; that He helps Jew, Muhammadan, and Christian alike.

Neither 'Abdu'l-Bahá nor His Father, Bahá'u'lláh, were ever taught the learning of men. Yet scientific men from different parts of the world go to question and inquire of 'Abdu'l-Bahá about many and various matters. Learned men, priests of the different systems, and even those in authority go to consult with Him; all regard Him as their friend and adviser.

Friday mornings at seven there is another picture. Near the tent in the garden one may see an assemblage of the abject poor—the lame, the halt, and the blind—seldom less than a hundred. As 'Abdu'l-Bahá passes among them He will be seen to give to each a small coin, and to add a word of sympathy or cheer; often an inquiry about those at home; frequently He sends a share to an absent one. It is a sorry procession as they file slowly away, but they all look forward to this weekly visit, and indeed it is said that this is the chief means of sustenance for some of them. Almost any morning, early, He may be seen making the round of the city, calling upon the feeble and the sick; many dingy abodes are brightened by His presence.

In 'Akká the little birds fly right into the rooms. The door of the dining room was usually open, and we frequently saw them eating crumbs from the table. The evening meal is at nine, after the custom of the Persians, and it is then that 'Abdu'l-Bahá talks and teaches. The following is the substance of what He said to us during one meal:

"Since the beginning of the world up to the present time, whenever a Manifestation or a Holy One appeared, all stood against Him, disgracefully treated Him, rejected and opposed Him, persecuted His followers, plundered their possessions, and at last sentenced Him to death, saying, 'This man (the Manifestation) is the cause of corrupting our laws and of destroying our religion.'

"They called Jesus a liar. But, notwithstanding all these afflictions which fell upon Him, He won the victory and subdued all to His Command; His spiritual authority prevailed in the world, and the deniers and those who contradicted Him failed and were frustrated. Though but few persons accepted and were converted in the Day of each one of the Manifestations, yet these few surpassed and overcame great multitudes. During the time of Christ only a few souls believed in Him, but they were so powerful in spirit that none of the learned men among the Israelites could resist and stand against them, and afterward their light illumined the world, their call was raised abroad, their stars twinkled in heaven, their diadem became resplendent, and they are shining with great brilliancy.

"When Christ passed away, He had eleven disciples. The greatest among them was Peter, and he denied Christ three times, but when Bahá'u'lláh departed He had a hundred thousand believers who were calling out 'Yá Bahá'u'l-Abhá' while they were under swords and daggers, and in these late years many men and women in Yazd were killed by inches without uttering a single cry or complaint, but rather called out the Greatest Name. From these incidents we may judge the future of this Revelation."

During our last meal, 'Abdu'l-Bahá broke a quantity of bread into His bowl; then asking for the plates of the pilgrims, He gave to each of us a portion. When the meal was finished, He said: "I have given you to eat from My bowl—now distribute My Bread among the people."

When we left 'Akká, we drove to the Tomb of Bahá'u'lláh, about two miles beyond the city. It is a small stone building of simplest construction, in a little garden of flowers. The gardener filled our arms with roses and carnations. From here, we visited the beautiful garden of "Riḍván," where Bahá'u'lláh so often went, sometimes remaining days at a time. As we were leaving, Abú'l-Qázim, the gardener, followed us across the little bridge and gave us some beautiful flowers, after which he climbed up on the wheel of the carriage and gave me a parting embrace. The "Riḍván" is in reality an island, and on both sides flow streams of clear water.

At unexpected places along the road we were surprised to again see the good faces of those we thought we had left behind, and once more they bade us good-bye.

Three days later, we left Haifa by steamer

THE RIḌVÁN GARDEN
in the Holy Land.

for Jaffa, from where we traveled fifty-four miles by narrow-gauge railroad up to Jerusalem. During the two days there we visited both Bethlehem and the Mount of Olives. We then returned to Jaffa for steamer to Port Said and went at once to Cairo, where we remained a week visiting the friends. We found here also that love and kindness which everywhere characterizes the Bahá'ís of the Orient. From Cairo we went to Alexandria, where we took a steamer for Naples.

'Abdu'l-Bahá had told us that He would be glad if we could arrange to visit the friends in Paris and London on our way home. Therefore, after traveling through Italy and Switzerland, we went to Paris, where we remained a week and attended several interesting meetings. We also were in London a week, and there met our American friends who were returning from India, where for several months they had been teaching in this Cause.

This is the account of our journey by land and water to 'Abdu'l-Bahá, but the true Journey and the real Meeting is of the spirit, for only that "cup" which one carries there is filled.

The only claim of 'Abdu'l-Bahá is the "Station of Servitude." As to His personality, He commands us to see the Light, not the Lamp.

"Blessed are those who know."

Roy.

A recent letter from Ḥaydar-'Alí, an old man of seventy-four years, whom we met and who was exiled and imprisoned for twelve years, two of them in chains, for his belief in this Revelation, has as its closing paragraph the following:

"May God speed the day when the limitations of personalities, prejudices of boundaries, and distinctions of the East, West, North, and South be entirely removed and all of us become true Bahá'ís."

Memories of 'Abdu'l-Bahá

1908 : 1910 : 1912 : 1913

by Stanwood Cobb

STANWOOD COBB
in later years.

I FIRST MET 'Abdu'l-Bahá vicariously, so to speak, and it was this meeting that brought me into the Bahá'í Faith in the summer of 1906. It happened that being in the vicinity of Green Acre* that summer I made a pilgrimage there to see what it was all about. My curiosity had been aroused by weekly articles in the *Boston Transcript*. At this time, I was studying for the Unitarian ministry at the Harvard Divinity School.

It was a warm Sunday afternoon in August. The big tent on Green Acre's lower level,

---

*The Green Acre conferences at Eliot, Maine, established by Sarah Farmer during 1894, in the aftermath of the Chicago World's Parliament of Religions, were devoted to the tolerant study of comparative religions and progressive ideas. After 1900, when Miss Farmer became a believer, Bahá'í teachers were included among the speakers.—ED.

where the lecture hall now is located, was filled to capacity to hear some famous sculptor from New York. I was not greatly interested in his lecture. It was not for the sake of art that I had come, but for the sake of religion.

At the end of the lecture I went up to speak to Sarah Farmer—who had been presiding in her own ineffable way, shedding a warm spiritual glow upon the whole affair. As I had previously met her in Cambridge at the home of Mrs. Ole Bull, I ventured to recall myself to her.

Miss Farmer took my hand in hers and cordially held it while she looked into my eyes and asked, "Have you heard of the Persian Revelation?"

"No," I answered.

"Well, go to that lady in the white headdress and ask her to tell you about it. I know by your eyes that you are ready for it."

What had she seen in my eyes? I do not know. But what she had read there proved true. For within half an hour from that moment I became a confirmed Bahá'í and have remained so ever since.

But it is of 'Abdu'l-Bahá that I am writing, and not of myself. How did it happen that

'Abdu'l-Bahá, seven thousand miles away and a prisoner in 'Akká, could at such a distance confirm me with such immediacy into the Bahá'í Faith?

It happened in this way. The path had been prepared, so to speak. For in reviewing books for the *Boston Transcript* which dealt with the prevailing and rapidly increasing flaws in our present civilization, and the need of a better world order, I had begun to debate deeply with myself on this matter of such great universal concern.

It is true, I thought, that a new and better pattern of civilization needs to be devised. But even if such a pattern—an ideal pattern—were conceived, who could put it over? Could I, as a clergyman, hope to convert all my congregation to it? Much less could I hope to convert the whole country. And no human being could by any conceivable power of vision and of personality bring all humanity into such a kingdom of perfection.

I still vividly remember how I was taking a long walk in the beautiful suburb of Chestnut Hill, around the reservoir, when the solution of this problem flashed into my mind. Someone must appear with more than human authority, in order to win the allegiance of the whole world to an ideal pattern for humanity.

This was my general frame of mind when Mary Lucas, the "woman in white"—a singer just back from visiting 'Abdu'l-Bahá—took me under an apple tree on the sloping lawn and proceeded to unfold to me the Persian Revelation. Her exposition was very simple. It consisted of only these four words: "Our Lord has come!"

The moment Mary Lucas uttered those words I felt, *This is it!* How did it happen that I felt that way? The "woman in white" had not discoursed to me upon the spiritual character and greatness of 'Abdu'l-Bahá, nor upon the principles of the Bahá'í Faith. How great is the power of speech, when one simple utterance could sweep me—mind, heart, and soul—into that Faith!

But it was more than these four words that empowered Mary Lucas so to usher me into the Cause. It was more than speech itself. It was a unique spiritual vibration which Mary Lucas had brought from 'Akká that convinced me. And it was the strange cosmic dynamism with which her words were charged that moved my soul.

If 'Abdu'l-Bahá Himself had stood under that apple tree and addressed me, I could not have been more convinced. For what is distance on the plane of spirit? Mary Lucas had brought the spirit of 'Abdu'l-Bahá with her. I felt it, and I was convinced. Especially as my own soul had already sought out and found the answer to the world's dire needs: *Someone must appear with more than human authority.*

So that was my first meeting with 'Abdu'l-Bahá—strangely vicarious, perhaps predestined. The second meeting—with 'Abdu'l-Bahá in person while He was still a prisoner in 'Akká —took place in the following way. In February of 1908, I had the great privilege of visiting Him in company with Lua Getsinger, famous in the annals of Bahá'í history.

I accidentally (or was it by destiny?) ran into Lua on the steps of Shepard Hotel in Cairo, where I had gone for a few days of travel during the midyear holidays of Robert College (Constantinople), in which at that time I was teacher of English and Latin.

"What are you doing here?" asked Lua in great surprise.

"What are *you* doing here?" I asked, in equal surprise.

It seems that Lua was on a pilgrimage to 'Akká, and she urged me to leave off my travels in Egypt and join her. I explained that I had written 'Abdu'l-Bahá for permission to visit, but had been answered that at that time it was not advisable.

"But I have standing permission to take anyone with me," urged Lua.

"But I have arranged a trip up the Nile with my friend."

"What is a trip up the Nile compared with the privilege of visiting the Master?"

Lua's logic was convincing and her ardor compelling. Twenty-four hours later saw me ensconced in a room adjoining 'Abdu'l-Bahá's in the historic "prison of 'Akká," in reality a large compound enclosed within walls.

My first meeting with 'Abdu'l-Bahá was bewildering. We were ushered into a long study, lighted by large French windows at the farther end. I saw a large desk there, but no person sitting at it. Only a radiance of light. As we approached the end of the room, a majestic figure in Oriental garb became evident to me. It was 'Abdu'l-Bahá.

Lua Getsinger, with the devotion of a Mary Magdalene, fell to her knees and fervently kissed His robe. But what was I to do? I am not one who can act insincerely. Should I merely shake hands with Him? As I stood in hesitation 'Abdu'l-Bahá, fully realizing my predicament, saved me from it by taking me in His arms and embracing me.

"You are welcome!" He said.

Every evening at dinner 'Abdu'l-Bahá, who did not eat at that time, helped to serve us. He went around from guest to guest, putting more food upon the plates. This is the height of Oriental hospitality, to serve an honored guest with one's own hands.

When the meal was over, 'Abdu'l-Bahá would give us a brief talk on spiritual themes. I regret I have not a memory sufficient to recall all that He said. But I do recall two of these messages of spiritual wisdom.

"It is not enough to wish to do good. The wish should be followed by action. What would you think of a mother who said, 'How I love you, my babe!'—yet did not give it milk? Or of a penniless man, who said, 'I am going to found a great university!'"

On another occasion, He spoke of the need for loving patience in the face of aggravating behavior on the part of others. "One might say, 'Well, I will endure such-and-such a person so long as he is endurable.' *But Bahá'ís must endure people even when they are unendurable.*"

Three extraordinary qualities which characterized all of 'Abdu'l-Bahá's utterances were to be found in these two brief conversations: His supreme logic; His delightful sense of humor; and the inspiring buoyancy with which He gave forth solemn pronouncements.

For instance, when He said, "But Bahá'ís must endure people even when they are unendurable," He did not look at us solemnly as if appointing us to an arduous and difficult task. Rather, He beamed upon us delightfully, as if to suggest what a joy to us it would be to act in this way!

I want to emphasize this important point—the joyousness with which 'Abdu'l-Bahá always depicted the spiritual life as He enjoined it upon us. And why not? Is man's spiritual life

'ABDU'L-BAHÁ

not in reality more joyous than any other kind of life that he can lead?

This philosophy of joy was the keynote of all of 'Abdu'l-Bahá's teaching. "Are you happy?" was His frequent greeting to his visitors. "Be happy!"

Those who were unhappy (and who of us are not at times!) would weep at this. And 'Abdu'l-Bahá would smile as if to say, "Yes, weep on. Beyond the tears is sunshine."

And sometimes He would wipe away with His own hands the tears from their wet cheeks, and they would leave His presence transfigured.

On the occasion of this visit I had been under a severe strain at Robert College, due to disciplinary troubles. That was one of the reasons for my diversionary trip to Egypt. Also, I had been slowly recovering in previous years from a nervous depression due to overwork at Dartmouth. I had been earning my way through Dartmouth, and also at the Harvard Divinity School. At times I would feel so depressed that I should have been glad to have found a hole in the ground, crawled into it, and pulled the hole in after me. I understood at such times the Hindu craving for extinction.

'Abdu'l-Bahá came into my room one morning without His translator. He sat beside me and took one of my hands in both of His and held it for a minute or two. He had not at any time inquired as to my health. He knew. From that moment on I found myself permanently relieved of these depressive moods. No matter how hard the going, I have always since then been glad to be alive.

At last, all too soon, the time came to go. The three days assigned for our visit had come to an end. I shall never forget how Lua Getsinger sobbed as if her heart would break as she slowly descended the long flight of steps, looking back frequently at 'Abdu'l-Bahá who stood benignly at the top.

And I shall never forget how joyously 'Abdu'l-Bahá smiled at Lua's tears, knowing that they were more precious than pure gold. For they were the complete offering, at that moment, of Lua's heart and soul to the Master—the instinctive expression of her great love. 'Abdu'l-Bahá knew that these were not tragic tears. They were like the vernal showers that prelude the rich blossoming of spring.

Needless to say, the ensuing spring at Robert College was one of the most glorious periods of my life. Never had the birds sung so sweetly, the flowers and shrubs bloomed so exquisitely, the golden sunshine seemed so intoxicating. As for my disciplinary troubles at the college, they vanished like mist which the sunshine dispels. My pupils, some of whom had been carrying knives and revolvers, loved me again and more than ever. Such was the magic power that I brought from 'Akká.

Again it was my privilege to visit 'Abdu'l-Bahá in the summer of 1910, and this time at His own invitation. I was given the privilege of spending a week there, in the Persian guest house on the slopes of Mt. Carmel. 'Abdu'l-Bahá at this time was living in Haifa in the home built for Him by Mrs. Jackson, having been freed from His imprisonment by the Young Turks in the summer of 1908. The oppressive and cruel governor who had in vain sought graft from Him and had threatened to send Him to the malign dungeons of Tunis, had himself met the fate he had designed for 'Abdu'l-Bahá—the fate of death, and at the hands of the Young Turks. And 'Abdu'l-Bahá was enjoying, for the first time since His boyhood, the luxury of freedom.

He seemed to me more noble in countenance, more regal in bearing, more potent in the power of His presence than ever before. Every evening at sunset He met with the pilgrims, assembled in a large room, and gave a spiritual discourse.

One afternoon, I found the pilgrims waiting outside at the gate for 'Abdu'l-Bahá. He had been making a call upon the Turkish consul and was expected soon. After a few moments we saw His carriage stop at the foot of the short hill, where He got out in order to walk the rest of the way for the sake of exercise. All of the Persian pilgrims stood in their customary reverential attitude, awaiting His approach with bowed heads and arms crossed upon their breasts. I alone, as an American, took the privilege of watching Him as He approached, enjoying the majesty of His movements and the nobility of His whole appearance. But as He neared me, I involuntarily also bowed my head. Some power emanating from Him seemed to obligate this attitude. So had Professor E. G. Browne, the only Occidental ever to visit Bahá'-

u'lláh, felt obligated to bow his head in the presence of the Prophet.*

This power emanating from 'Abdu'l-Bahá was not expressed for the purpose of producing submission. It was a power which He never expressed to non-Bahá'ís. Let us say, rather, that it was a privilege He gave us, of seeing a little behind the veil; of experiencing the direct effect of that Cosmic Power which in this early period of our development seems supernormal, however normal it may become to us at some distant future stage of our soul's development.

No, 'Abdu'l-Bahá never put forth any of His spiritual power to dazzle, persuade, or overawe sceptics or unbelievers. Of this fact I shall later give a vivid instance.

On the day I arrived at Haifa I was ill with a dysentery which I had picked up in the course

---

*Professor Browne was not the only Westerner ever to visit Bahá'u'lláh, but he wrote the famous pen portrait which includes the following description of his first meeting with Him: "No need to ask in whose presence I stood, as I bowed myself before one who is the object of a devotion and love which kings might envy and emperors sigh for in vain!"—ED.

of my travels. 'Abdu'l-Bahá sent His own physician to me, and visited me Himself. He said, "I would that I could take your illness upon myself." I have never forgotten this. I felt, I knew, that in making this remark 'Abdu'l-Bahá was not speaking in mere terms of sympathy. He meant just what He said.

Such is the great love of the Kingdom, of which 'Abdu'l-Bahá spoke so often and so much. This is a love which is difficult, almost impossible, for us to acquire—though we may seek to approximate its perfection. It is more than sympathy, more than empathy. It is sacrificial love.

Looking back, it seems strange that 'Abdu'l-Bahá did not employ His healing power directly upon me, as He had done on the occasion of my previous visit. He left me to the care of His physician and to the prescribed medications. It took three days for me to get on my feet again.

Why did He not restore me directly to health by means of spiritual healing? There is some deep spiritual lesson here. It was not 'Abdu'l-Bahá's province to go about healing physical diseases. It was His mission to expound the Teachings and express the spiritual potency of the world's Divine Physician. Physical events and conditions are of less importance in our lives than the development of our spiritual nature.

In regard to health in general, I will quote here a statement which 'Abdu'l-Bahá had made to me on my previous visit: that health is the expression of equilibrium; that the body is composed of certain elements, and that when these elements are in the right proportion, health results; and that if there is any lack or preponderance in these elements, sickness results.

Thus, fifty years ago, 'Abdu'l-Bahá gave in a simple statement to me all the truths which the new science of biochemistry is now discovering.

But there is still another cause of illness, 'Abdu'l-Bahá went on to say. Illness may be caused by nervous factors. Anything that shocks us or affects our nerves may also affect our health.

All that has been written up to this point is a sort of introduction to the recording of my memories of 'Abdu'l-Bahá on the occasion of His visit to this country in 1912. The purpose of this introduction is to show what sort of a personage it was that on April 11, 1912, landed at the port of New York for an extended visit and lecture tour in this country.

Here was an Oriental in Oriental garb, a man who had been prisoner most of His life, a character whose life was for the most part lived on a spiritual plane so lofty as to be almost beyond our comprehension. How did this Servant of God meet, fit into, and adjust to the objective, dynamic, and materialistic life of America?

'Abdu'l-Bahá, upon landing in New York and being surrounded by alert and inquisitive reporters, was perfectly at home. And why not? Is there any limit to the power of spirit? Was not 'Abdu'l-Bahá's universal spirit as capable of dealing with the fast-vibrating technological Occident as it had been in dealing with the mystic and more spiritual Orient? We shall see, as this narrative continues, how He was "all things to all men"; protean in His universality; thoroughly at home in every environment.

This majestic figure—in tarboosh, turban, and flowing robes—drew the newspaper men into His aura and immediately won their favor.

"What do you think of America?" He was asked.

"I like it. Americans are optimistic. If you ask them how they are they say 'All right!' If you ask them how things are going, they say, 'All right!' This cheerful attitude is good."

And so 'Abdu'l-Bahá won reporters' hearts and continued to do so throughout His stay in America. He never seemed to them, or was described by them, as a strange or exotic personality. He always received favorable and constructive notices from the press.

For eight months 'Abdu'l-Bahá traveled over the United States from coast to coast, giving addresses in churches, universities, and lecture halls. Several of these addresses I was privileged to attend. As I look back on these occasions, I recall more vividly His platform presence than the contents of His addresses, which of course have all been published.*

'Abdu'l-Bahá did not, as a lecturer, stand still. His movements were very dynamic. He paced back and forth on the platform as He gave forth His spiritual utterances. I felt that the general atmosphere and the effect of His

---

*See *The Promulgation of Universal Peace* (Chicago: Bahá'í Publishing Committee, 1922–25), Second Edition (Wilmette, Ill.: Bahá'í Publishing Trust, 1982).—ED.

'ABDU'L-BAHÁ WITH THE BAHÁ'ÍS in Lincoln Park, Chicago. May 5, 1912.

words were enhanced rather than diminished by the presence of a translator. For the techniques of translation gave 'Abdu'l-Bahá a certain spiritual dignity, such as could not have been attained by a straight address in the language of His hearers.

The situation was as follows: 'Abdu'l-Bahá would make a statement of a length within the power of the translator to render; then He would stand and smile as the translation was given, or He would nod His head to affirm important points. In other words, 'Abdu'l-Bahá did not stand passive during the period of translation. He constantly illumined this translation with the dynamic power of His own spiritual personality.

And when He spoke, the Persian words—so beautiful and strong—boomed forth almost as musically as in operatic recitatives. While He spoke He was in constant and majestic motion. To hear Him was an experience unequaled in any other kind of platform delivery. It was a work of art, as well as a spiritual service. First would come this spiritual flow of thought musically expressed in a foreign tongue. Then, as the translator set forth its meaning to us, we had the added pleasure of watching 'Abdu'l-Bahá's response to the art of the translator. It was, all in all, a highly colorful and dramatic procedure.

The substance of 'Abdu'l-Bahá's talks, here and in London and Paris, have been published and are available for study.* One can perceive in all of these addresses and discussions a peculiar adaptation to the Occidental mentality and way of thinking. They are, to sum it up in one word, supremely logical.

It was the Greeks who taught the world how to think in logical terms, and they thereby laid the foundation for all Western thought and science. From the Greeks we have learned how to begin at "A" in order to get to "Z"—or as in Greek, from "Alpha" to "Omega."

The Orientals do not think in just this way. Their mentality has never submitted to the Greek discipline. Their minds are more mystical, more immediate in perception. They do not have to begin at "A" in order to comprehend

―――――――
*See *Paris Talks* (London: Bahá'í Publishing Trust, 1912 [1969]) and *'Abdu'l-Bahá in London* (London, Bahá'í Publishing Trust, 1912 [1987]).—ED.

the station of "Z." Through spiritual sensitivity, through rapid intuitional processes, they can often gain an immediate awareness or comprehension of the ultimate—of the "Omega" itself.

All Oriental seers and prophets speak oracularly. One sentence, one paragraph will contain a wealth which a lifetime of thought cannot exhaust. Christ spoke this way. Bahá'u'lláh spoke this way.

But 'Abdu'l-Bahá, for the sake of the Western world, adopted the Greek mode of presentation, carefully elaborating His theses and developing them from known and admissible premises. In no place is 'Abdu'l-Bahá ever obscure or recondite. If He wishes to present a great spiritual truth, He takes it up at an initial point where its truth will be acknowledged by all, and then develops it into a larger presentation such as can expand our very minds and souls.

And so, whatever else 'Abdu'l-Bahá was and in the future will be realized to be, it is recognizable even today that He was God's special gift to the Occident. He translated the oracular teachings of Bahá'u'lláh into a language and form easily comprehensible to the West. So

'ABDU'L-BAHÁ IN AMERICA

that no one, having available these lucid pronouncements of 'Abdu'l-Bahá, can say that the Bahá'í Faith is hard to understand. 'Abdu'l-Bahá has set forth its Teachings with all the lucidity of daylight and the warmth of sunlight.

Regarding the countless personal interviews which the Master gave to Bahá'ís and non-Bahá'ís alike, volumes could be written. I will tell here only of the interviews which I personally was privileged to have.

When 'Abdu'l-Bahá was in Boston, I seized this opportunity to take my father in to see Him, from our home in the suburb of Newton. Father at that time was a venerable Boston artist seventy-five years of age—an earnestly religious man, devout, spiritual, and prayerful. He was sympathetic to my adherence to the Bahá'í Cause, but he had said, "Son, I am too old to change." While I was in Constantinople, Father had at my request attended some of the Bahá'í meetings in Boston; and now he was glad to have this opportunity to visit with 'Abdu'l-Bahá.

But what was my consternation to perceive that Father was taking the conversation into his own hands! It was an occurrence which I never shall forget. Father for some half-hour proceeded to lay down the law to 'Abdu'l-Bahá, or let us say, to enlighten Him on spiritual themes. Or to be more exact, let us say that Father took this opportunity to express to the loving, listening ear of 'Abdu'l-Bahá the spiritual philosophy which had guided him in life.

I sat there quite shocked. But I didn't need to be. 'Abdu'l-Bahá plainly was not shocked at this reversal of the customary role—He now to be the listener and His visitor the discourser. He sat there smiling, saying little, enveloping us with His love. And at the end, Father came away feeling that he had had a wonderful interview. What a lesson in humility this was, that 'Abdu'l-Bahá thus exemplified! There are so many times when we can help others best just by being good listeners.

The last interview I had in this country with 'Abdu'l-Bahá was in Washington. Strange, that I do not recall what He said. My heart was too full to take any notes! I only can recall how He embraced me at the end, kissed me, and said three times: *"Be on fire with the love of the Kingdom!"*

What is this "love of the Kingdom"? That is what humanity must henceforward spend a

'ABDU'L-BAHÁ.
Taken at Dublin, New Hampshire, in 1912.

few thousand years to discover and apply to life. Did 'Abdu'l-Bahá mean the love *for* the Kingdom or the kind of love *that prevails in* the Higher Kingdom? Or did He mean both these loves?

Here in these nine words 'Abdu'l-Bahá summed up the gist of all His teaching; which was that love, applied by means of the Holy Spirit, is the one thing that will solve all problems of man, both as an individual and as a collective society.

The most important interview I had with 'Abdu'l-Bahá was in Paris in the spring of 1913. I was one of the staff of Porter Sargent's Travel School for Boys. On my first visit He inquired about the school and asked me what I taught. I told Him that I taught English, Latin, algebra, and geometry. He gazed intently at me with His luminous eyes and said, "Do you teach the spiritual things?"

This question embarrassed me. I did not know how to explain to 'Abdu'l-Bahá that the

'ABDU'L-BAHÁ IN PARIS
near the Eiffel Tower.

necessity of preparing the boys for college entrance exams dominated the nature of the curriculum. So I simply answered: "No, there is not time for that."

'Abdu'l-Bahá made no comment on this answer. But He did not need to. Out of my own mouth I had condemned myself and modern education. *No time for spiritual things!* That, of course, is just what is wrong with our modern materialistic "civilization." It has no time to give for spiritual things.

But 'Abdu'l-Bahá's question and His silent response indicated that from His viewpoint spiritual things should come first. And why not? The material world, as the expression of man's spirit, is subordinate to the spiritual world. Therefore, education should begin with that which is primary and causal; and not with that which, as the creation of man, is secondary to his creative spirit and to the Creative Spirit of the cosmos.

'Abdu'l-Bahá kindly invited me to bring Porter Sargent and the pupils to see Him. Mr. Sargent gladly accepted the invitation, and four of the boys did. The others had excuses, like those people in the Bible who were invited to the wedding feast but did not go. One boy had to buy a pair of shoes; another had planned to take afternoon tea at a restaurant where a gypsy orchestra furnished music, et cetera. How many of life's important opportunities thus pass us by, through our own unperceptiveness or neglect!

I was deeply interested and concerned to see what impression 'Abdu'l-Bahá would make on the owner of the school. Porter Sargent, ten years my senior, was a confirmed and positive atheist. He had been a biologist, and was suffering from that spiritual myopia which so often afflicts this type of scientist. But he was an idealist, a humanitarian, a man of great vision for humanity, and somewhat of a genius.

In one intimate discussion with me on the nature of existence, during a long hike we took together on the sunny island of Capri, he had outlined to me his concept of life and the universe.

"What do you think of it?" he asked me, with some eagerness. Perhaps this was the first occasion on which he had so fully expounded his philosophy of life.

"It is splendid!" I said. "But it only covers half of existence."

"What is the other half?"

'ABDU'L-BAHÁ WITH BAHÁ'ÍS IN PARIS.

"Spirit."

But this other half did not exist for Porter Sargent. Idealist that he was, creative-minded, somewhat of a poet—I felt sad that not one ray of spirit could penetrate the pride of his intellect.

So when this golden opportunity came of an interview with 'Abdu'l-Bahá, I had great hopes. Now, in this intimate meeting with the Master, I thought, Sargent will be forced to realize the existence of spirit. 'Abdu'l-Bahá's spiritual potency will at last penetrate his shell of skepticism.

And so, when we came out from the hotel after a half-hour conference with 'Abdu'l-Bahá, I eagerly asked, "Well, what do you think of Him?"

I have never forgotten my shattering disappointment at the answer: "He's a dear, kind, tired old man."

I was chagrined. But this experience taught me two spiritual lessons. The first was that skepticism must solve its own problems, in its own way. The second truth, even more important, was that Spirit never forces itself upon the individual. It must be invited.

Theologians have frequently made the observation that God could easily force us to reverence and stand in awe of Him, if He wished. But He does not wish to win man's reverence and awe and love by any forceful way. The initiative must come from man himself.

And so, in the case of 'Abdu'l-Bahá, I noticed upon many occasions that He never expressed spiritual power for the purpose of dazzling people, or of winning them to a spiritual allegiance for which they were not inwardly prepared. The greater the receptivity of the individual, the greater was the revelation of spiritual potency which 'Abdu'l-Bahá displayed.

Thus Juliet Thompson, who painted 'Abdu'l-Bahá's portrait, has testified to the glorious revelations of Himself which her Subject at times made to her. In similar vein have testified the Kinneys, with whom 'Abdu'l-Bahá spent several weeks. And May Maxwell once told me that she had received, upon one sacred occasion in the presence of 'Abdu'l-Bahá, such a revelation of Him that she would never attempt to describe it.

But materially-minded people 'Abdu'l-Bahá met upon their own plane, as He did Porter Sargent. And as I also saw Him do in Washington with the Turkish ambassador, on the occasion of Mrs. Parson's reception. This being a social affair, 'Abdu'l-Bahá did not play the part of the Master, but the part of a guest amenable to the situation. And anyone who had looked into the large reception room, as I did, and had seen 'Abdu'l-Bahá sitting in a corner and exchanging funny stories with the ambassador, would have seen in 'Abdu'l-Bahá's facial expressions no trace of spiritual power. For He was not here primarily for spiritual purposes, but to play a social part.

'Abdu'l-Bahá was indeed "all things to all men." He was protean. If some were prepared only to see Him as the Old Man of the Sea, such He was to them. But if they were prepared to see Him as more than this, the degree of their receptivity was proportionately blessed.

In all my interviews with 'Abdu'l-Bahá I had an extraordinary feeling of receiving truth from a higher plane than that of the mere intellect. Man's intellect is an organ of discrimination, an instrument for analysis and attack. As we listen to other people more learned than ourselves, we are pleased to get information, but we consciously reserve the right of judgment. Some of the things said to us we accept immediately; some with reservations; and some we inwardly oppose. No matter how wise or how learned the teacher, we reserve the right of our own judgment.

But with 'Abdu'l-Bahá it was different. I accepted always His statements with humility and with total conviction; not because of any assumption of authority, but because I always felt in the depths of my soul that what He said was truth. It always *rang true*, so to speak. Let us say, as it was said of another great leader of men, that He spoke "with authority."

In the course of His lectures here and abroad 'Abdu'l-Bahá discoursed on many subjects. Where did He get His wide knowledge of things and of affairs? He had had but one year of schooling at the age of seven. He had been a prisoner all His life. He had few books, no scholarly library, no encyclopedias.

Yet at Schenectady, as 'Abdu'l-Bahá was being shown around the General Electric Works by Steinmetz, this "wizard of electricity" was observed to be eagerly absorbing 'Abdu'l-Bahá's elucidation of electricity. The Rev. Moore, Unitarian clergyman who was present at the time, testified to me: "Steinmetz's jaw seemed to drop open as he drank in 'Abdu'l-Bahá's talk."

"'Abdu'l-Bahá, do You know everything?" Saffa Kinney is said to have asked.
"No, I do not know everything. But when I need to know something, it is pictured before Me."

And so 'Abdu'l-Bahá, on the occasion of His tour of the General Electric Works, knew more about electricity than did Steinmetz.

Shoghi Effendi has said that intuition is a power of the soul. It was this power that was always available to 'Abdu'l-Bahá, and available in its totality. He has spoken many times of this "immediate knowledge"—this knowledge attained without the means of books or other humans, this strange intuitive power which to some degree is available to us all.

And often, in closing an interview after answering some abstruse question, 'Abdu'l-Bahá would say: "Time does not permit of further answer. But meditate on this, and truth will come to you."

And so—although 'Abdu'l-Bahá is no longer

with us to answer our questions—the power of the Holy Spirit so strong in Him is still available to us to guide, to fortify, to heal.

I have tried to describe 'Abdu'l-Bahá as I saw and knew Him. But how can anyone give an adequate description of this personality that, like St. Paul, was all things to all men?

The Persian doctor who attended Him from 1914 till His death, when recently asked at a meeting in Milwaukee to describe 'Abdu'l-Bahá, replied that this was very difficult to do; because 'Abdu'l-Bahá expressed Himself differently at different times, meeting every occasion as the occasion demanded.

If one were asked to describe 'Abdu'l-Bahá in a single word, that word would be: "protean." This unusual adjective is derived from the name of a minor deity in Greek mythology who had the magic power to assume any form he wished. And so 'Abdu'l-Bahá could be on one occasion all love; on another occasion supreme wisdom; and on other rare occasions, expressing a power that seemed cosmic.

And since love, wisdom, and power are the three principles upon which the Cosmos is run; and since 'Abdu'l-Bahá was designated as our exemplar, it follows that these qualities should be developed in us all, as we grow spiritually toward the attainment of our full stature as citizens of that Kingdom of God destined to be the consumation of our planetary existence.

What was the secret of 'Abdu'l-Bahá's power? He suggests the answer in His own words.

"The human body is in need of material force, but the spirit has need of the Holy Spirit. If it is aided by the bounty of the Holy Spirit it will attain great power; it will discover realities; it will be informed of the mysteries. The power of the Holy Spirit is here for all. The captive of the Holy Spirit is exempt from every captivity.

"The teachings of His Holiness Bahá'u'lláh are the breaths of the Holy Spirit which create man anew."

Whatever was and still is the reality of 'Abdu'l-Bahá, it is evident from the events of His life that He was endowed with a cosmic power for the fulfillment of His mission. Every unexpected circumstance, every event in the midst of the Occidental civilization so foreign to His own background, He met not only successfully but also with a power that won all hearts.

His directives to Bahá'ís always focused on the need of divine aid—the aid of Spirit—in order to exemplify and propagate the Bahá'í Faith and lay the foundations for that New World Order laid down by Bahá'u'lláh for the establishment of a spiritually motivated world civilization.

To those who would like to pursue further the marvelous details of 'Abdu'l-Bahá's life we recommend *Portals to Freedom* by Howard Ives,* a Unitarian clergyman prior to his conversion to Bahá'í. We had the pleasure of meeting Ives in New York in 1910, when he was at the beginning of his search for spiritual reality.

"Cobb, I'd like you to meet a young clergyman who is becoming interested in Bahá'í," said my friend Montfort Mills to me one day. "Can you have lunch with us tomorrow?"

I was glad to accept this invitation and to

*(London: George Ronald, 1937 [1962]).—ED.

meet an earnest seeker. I do not recall our conversation at the lunch table. But it was evident that Ives was seriously searching.

This meeting with Ives resulted on my part in a memorable friendship with a man who was destined ultimately to celebrate the personality and teachings of one who in 1912, became his Teacher and Master.

In his vivid narrative Howard Ives reports many loving meetings and interviews with 'Abdu'l-Bahá. The impression of this spiritual leader which remained a constant in Ives' recollections is expressed by him in the following words: "What 'Abdu'l-Bahá said impressed me with the force of the impact of Divine Truth. There was not a question in my mind of the authority with which He spoke."

A Week In
'Abdu'l-Bahá's Home

1920

by Genevieve L. Coy

GENEVIEVE COY
in later years.

"We have beheld the King in His Beauty; we have seen the land that is very far off."*

SEPTEMBER 1, 1920. Our party of four American pilgrims† had left Cairo on the evening of August 31st. Three of the Egyptian Bahá'ís had come to the train to bid us farewell, and to give us messages to take to Haifa. One of the group was an Armenian, who brought a basket of fruit for the Master. Another was Mírzá Tawfiq, a young man of twenty-one or -two years of age, who is a student in the college in Beirut. He interpreted for us often during our five days in Cairo, and also served as a most pleasant and helpful guide in some of our trips about the city. The third person to bid us Godspeed was Muḥammad-Taqí Iṣfahání, in whose

*Cf. Isaiah 33:17.—ED.
†The four pilgrims who made this glorious journey together were Mable Paine, Sylvia Paine, Cora Grey, and Genevieve Coy.—G.L.C.

home we had spent some of our happiest hours in Cairo. He speaks no English, but he gave us many sweet thoughts, through Mírzá Tawfiq's interpretation, and his smile was a benediction.

We loved him so much that we could not have borne parting from him had it not been that the goal of our journey was Haifa and the Master! His parting gift to us was a tray of delicious pastry and a lovely bouquet of roses. Through all the next day's ride the flowers kept fresh, and on the day after that there were two or three buds that were fresh enough to be given to the Master, when Mírzá Muḥammad-Taqí's message of love was told him. The Master wore them in his girdle all the rest of that day, and said that he always was happy when he thought of the loving heart of the Bahá'í who had given us the flowers.

When we woke on the morning of September 1st, the train was running through the desert country of southern Palestine. For mile after mile the rolling sand dunes stretched into the distance. Long lines of camels were passed; and occasionally acres of date palms, loaded with green dates, showed where a little moisture was held in the sand below the dry surface. For hours we looked out of the window, watching, with an intense fascination, those long miles of desert. Someone in our party said that she could quite understand why the children of Israel murmured in the wilderness, if that was the kind of country that they had to travel through! We wondered whether Joseph and Mary, and the infant Jesus, had traveled so hard a road when they went down into Egypt. But later, in Haifa, we were told that the tradition of the country says that they went to the port at the foot of Mt. Carmel, and from there continued their journey to Egypt by boat.

During the middle of the day, the train passed from the desert into the pasture land. That is as different from our green American meadows as one can imagine. The pastures are brown and dry, and we wondered how the many herds of goat and sheep that we saw could find enough food to keep them alive. We saw almost no cows, and in Haifa we found that it is very difficult to obtain milk; we did not see any butter while we were in Palestine. Instead of butter, a white, salty cheese made from goat's milk is served.

In the afternoon we rode through the beautiful valley near Jaffa, with its thousands and thousands of fruit trees. The fields have to be irrigated, but when that is done they "blossom abundantly," and the trees are loaded with oranges and lemons, which were green at that season of the year. A little farther north is the valley of Sharon, and we tried to remember some of the beautiful words of the Old Testament with regard to that valley. "The wilderness and the solitary place shall be glad for them; and the desert shall rejoice and blossom as the rose. It shall blossom abundantly even with joy and singing; the glory of Lebanon shall be given unto it, the excellency of Carmel and Sharon, they shall see the *glory of the Lord* and the excellency of our God."*

The last part of the journey was very beautiful. The train ran close to the edge of the seashore, and we saw the sun drop down through fleecy clouds and sink in the blue waters of the Mediterranean. On the right, a low range of hills rose—rocky, and sparsely covered with vegetation. Beyond them appeared line after line of hills, until, far in the distance, high blue mountains towered into the sky. We thought that they must be the Lebanons, and we wondered whether we should soon see the valley of

---

*Isaiah 35:1–2.—ED.

A WEEK IN 'ABDU'L-BAHÁ'S HOME

'Akká. After a time, the lowest range of hills rose so close that all the others were blotted out. Cora suggested that perhaps the termination of this range was Mt. Carmel, and so it proved to be, for suddenly we rounded a point of land, and Haifa appeared to the east, with Mt. Carmel above.

Haifa lies on a narrow plain at the foot of the mountain, but there are buildings scattered part way up the slope. A long white road traverses the length of the hill, and reaches the top near its western extremity. I looked for the Tomb of the Báb, but I am not sure whether I saw it then. The train runs through a considerable part of the town, before reaching the station, and our eyes were very eager in their search for the various places of which we had heard so much. Suddenly, I remembered that we should now be able to see 'Akká across the bay, and hurrying to the other side of the car, I looked out—and across the water I glimpsed the city of the Lord, the "door of hope." We were so happy to be so near our journey's end —we were so full of expectation, that it seemed as if the train would never reach the station. But at last we did pull up in front of it!

Cora went out to look for a porter, and I was

HAIFA
the main street. The Shrine of the Báb is barely discernable, midway up the mountain.

ready to pass baggage out of the window to her. But almost immediately a hand was reached in to shake mine, and we were welcomed by a young man, whom we later learned was Rúhí Effendi, one of the Master's grandsons. Soon a familiar figure appeared in the car, Fujita, whom we had last seen in New York. He helped pass out bundles, and soon we were all on the platform with our numerous parcels and bags beside us. We shook hands with several young men, Bahá'ís from the Master's household, and then we four American pilgrims were in the auto, with the driver, Rúhí Effendi, and some of our baggage. Sa'íd Effendi, who had just arrived from Alexandria, Fujita and the other friends waited for the car to return for them.

The car ran through several streets, going steadily upwards—and I was too happy and too far from ordinary speech to be able to say a word. Suddenly we turned a corner, and after going less than a hundred yards the car stopped. I recognized the Pilgrim House, from the picture of it in *The Light of the World*.* On the

---

*A Bahá'í pilgrim's account by George O. Latimer (Boston: by the author, 1920).—ED.

THE SHRINE OF THE BÁB
during the time of 'Abdu'l-Bahá.

other side of the road was the wall of the Master's garden, and rising above it, the little room, like a watchtower, in which the Master often stays.

During our ride from the station, Rúhí Effendi told us that the Master was staying on the mountain for a few days, to rest from the many demands made on his time when he is in his house in the town. We would not see him until the next day. Perhaps we were disappointed for a moment, but here one knows that all the Master does is wisely done. And next morning, we were sure that it was well that we should have time to rest, and drink in the exquisite peace of the place, before meeting him.

At the door of the Pilgrim House, we were met by two Americans, Mrs. Hoagg and Malcolm McGillavrey. Malcolm had been in Haifa a week, but Mrs. Hoagg had been there since early in the summer. She acted as hostess for the Pilgrim House; she showed us to our rooms —one for Cora and me, another for Mabel and Sylvia. Simple, clean, and filled with a faint fragrance as of incense, is our place of rest, the place the Master has provided for those who come from the West. Every hour I wonder more at the love and kindness which has so provided for our comfort! Whenever we sit down to a meal, I think, "This is the meal the *Master* has given us!" The material food has come now, but the spiritual food had reached us in America!

Fujita cares for the house; he gets the breakfast; he serves the lunch, the food for which is brought over from the Master's house; he washes the dishes, he cleans the lamps, he is always busy in serving us. In the evening, he helps wait on table at dinner in the Master's house. The other boy who serves at dinner is K̲husraw, who came from Burma when he was very young, to serve the Master.

After our arrival at the Pilgrim House, we sat on the porch for a while. The night was beautiful—a full moon, and yet the stars were very bright. At about half past seven, Mrs. Hoagg took us over to the Master's house to meet the ladies of the household. We entered a gate that is covered with a luxuriant growth of vines, and walked under an arbor to the entrance of the house. It was hard to believe that we were really there! We had seen pictures of the house often, and it was so very like the pictures! (That is true of everything here. The pictures we have seen have been very good, I think, for one recognizes places and people immediately.)

A WEEK IN 'ABDU'L-BAHÁ'S HOME

We went up a rather long, broad flight of steps, turned to the left, and were in a high-ceilinged room of moderate size. There were many chairs and divans against the wall, and at the end of the room was a big wicker chair which one knew at once was the Master's. Immediately, the ladies came in. They greeted us with the Greatest Name, they inquired about our health, our journey, about the believers in America. Rúhí Effendi translated for those who did not speak English. There were present the Holy Mother,* the Greatest Holy Leaf,† two of the daughters,‡ Ṭúbá Khánum and Rúḥá Khánum; two or three young girls, granddaughters of the Master—and Fu'ad, the adorable four-year-old grandson, whose picture I had seen in Mr. Latimer's notebook.

The Holy Mother spoke about Bahá'u'lláh's commands about education. The two daughters talked with us about the friends in America. Little Fu'ád ran in and out on a very sturdy pair of legs. I cannot remember much of what was said. We knew that we were very welcome. We knew that we were at home as never

---

*Muníḿih Khánum, the wife of 'Abdu'l-Bahá
†Bahiyyih Khánum, the sister of 'Abdu'l-Bahá
‡That is, of 'Abdu'l-Bahá.

before! I could not but try to realize that *these* were the women who had been for years prisoners in 'Akká, who had undergone unspeakable hardships—these women with smiling faces who welcomed us so cordially.

After a time, how long I cannot tell, someone came and announced dinner. The ladies said good-night, for they do not come to the table where the men pilgrims are.* We were taken out into a big, big room which had a long table down the center. Many men came filing in and seated themselves. There were probably twenty or thirty at the table. Later, we learned that five religions and six or seven nationalities were represented. Christians, Muhammadans, Buddhists, Zoroastrians, Jews—were met in love and unity at the table of our Master. Egyptian, Persian, Arab, Burmese, Japanese, American, Parsee, Turk—and perhaps other nationalities were infinitely happy because they had found the joy that passeth understanding—because they were the guests of

---

*Of necessity, 'Abdu'l-Bahá's family observed the Muslim customs of veiling and social separation of the sexes during this time. Western women were not bound by these customs, of course.—ED.

'Abdu'l-Bahá! One does not remember words here, but the atmosphere of joy and peace is unforgettable.

As we were leaving the house, Rúhí Effendi, who had just come down from the mountain, brought word that the Master would either come down, or send for us the next day.

At the Pilgrim House, we sat out on the porch in the moonlight and talked until almost ten o'clock—and then went to our rooms to pass our first night in the Holy Land! I slept peacefully, and the night was all the more beautiful because I woke several times for a few minutes of happy realization that we were at last in Haifa, in the "land of heart's desire!"

SEPTEMBER 2, 1920. To waken in the Pilgrim House in Haifa is a very, very happy experience! From our west windows we could catch a glimpse of the Tomb of the Báb, and how eagerly we looked up at it, knowing that there the Master was dwelling; there was the memorial to the wonderful young herald of our Faith, the Supreme Báb.

Breakfast in the Pilgrim House comes at seven o'clock. It is a simple, friendly meal. The food consisted of tea, toast, poached eggs, honey, and cheese. And the lovely companionship of the friends! There were the seven of us who slept in the House, and Sa'íd Effendi and Mírzá Luṭfu'lláh always came in and had breakfast with us. Mírzá Luṭfu'lláh came down from the mountain each morning, bringing handfuls of jasmine blossoms from the garden of the Tomb, and these he strewed on the table. They were a lovely reminder of the spiritual fragrance of that spot!

After breakfast on that morning I was sitting in our room praying. Cora was writing at the table, the door into the living room was open and the various sounds of the household drifted in to us. I was having a very happy time reading some of the prayers in the little prayerbook, and also in praying for the friends who were not there with us. I found myself bathed in a wonderful atmosphere of love and peace. It was like nothing I had ever experienced! It was not supernatural in the sense of seeming queer or strange. It was simply an all-pervading peace and calm that seemed to fill my whole heart and spirit. I seemed to be at one with all the beauty and joy and light in the universe. Thus, I think, some ray of love from the Master's thought prepared me for meeting him that day.

At lunch, Rúhí Effendi brought word that we were to go up to the Tomb at about four in the afternoon, to see the Master! After lunch we all went and rested for an hour and a half. That is part of the day's program always. At three o'clock came tea, another invariable occurrence.

As the hour drew near when we were to go up the "Mountain of the Lord," to meet 'Abdu'l-Bahá, I remembered one evening we had spent with Juliet Thompson not long before we had left New York. She had said with deep earnestness, "When you are in the Master's presence, do not be self-conscious if you can help it. Do not be afraid. There is nothing to fear. He is all love and kindness. Pray, pray, all the way on your journey, that your hearts may be freed from all self-consciousness. Go to him, freely, gladly!"

I had tried to remember that, I had prayed for purity of heart that I might learn the lessons the Master will teach those who are ready to learn. And yet as we rode up the steep road toward the Tomb, there was a strange mixture of love and dread and longing in my heart. The way seemed very long! And yet it was very beautiful. We saw the valley of 'Akká, with the river Kishon winding through it down to the sea. Across the bay, 'Akká shone brightly in the afternoon sunlight—that "White Spot" which so many, many pilgrims have sought because the Glory of God had lived there.

Finally, we turned off from the main road, and the carriage drove down a steep incline toward the *musáfir-khánih*—the Persian Hospice for men. There we alighted and Mrs. Hoagg led us along a wide path, which is bordered with cypress trees on one side and with fig trees on the other. We passed the house of the caretaker, with the little room on top where the Master sometimes sleeps when He is on the mountain, and walked around to the front of the Tomb.

In front of the Tomb of the Báb, we found perhaps thirty of the men pilgrims sitting. One of the most majestic was a tall man, dressed in a long black robe—one of the Bahá'í teachers from 'Ishqábád. And with all his dignity, he had the most beautiful laughter-wrinkles around his eyes! One soon realized the cause of the latter, for he smiled almost all the time!

We were shown to seats in front of the Tomb, on the edge of the beautiful garden of the terrace. We were told that the Master would come soon. During the last few days, I had prayed so much for the ability to learn to serve the many children of the Father. I had found myself trying to imagine what the Master's presence would be like—and then had tried *not* to do that for fear I would be hindering my realization of his actual presence! And so I had tried to go to him with only the thought of the love of God in my heart.

Suddenly, all of the believers rose and faced the East. Then, from around the corner of the Tomb came the Master with two of the young men walking a little behind him. He came slowly toward us, and said, "Welcome, welcome!" in English; and then, "Sit down, sit down!" Sylvia sat next him; then Mabel Paine, myself, Cora, and Mrs. Hoagg. The other friends were beyond her, in two rows.

When the Master had walked toward us, it seemed to me that I had seen him come just that way at some previous time. He seemed to be so beautifully familiar to me! I suppose it must have seemed so because of the pictures I have seen of him, and the stories I have heard other pilgrims tell. It was a moment that one would prolong if one could, that one would never forget!

The Master began to speak in Persian, and Rúhí Effendi translated into English. He asked several questions; he talked of principles of living. Sometimes he would be silent for several minutes, with his eyes looking far, far away. It is very difficult to remember much of what he said. Indeed, it was almost difficult to *listen!*

I wished only to look and look at the beauty of his face! For that was what impressed me first—the exquisite beauty of the Master. It was like the most beautiful pictures we have of him, with life and color added. His is a face of living silver—the wonderful silver of hair and beard, and the blue of his eyes. The side face is majestic and sweet and loving. It was that which we saw most of the time. The full face is more dignified; to me it seemed more awe-inspiring. And yet, when he smiled, it was most exquisitely friendly, and human!

But he looked very, very tired. And one of the secretaries had said in the morning that he looked more rested than when he had gone up to the Tomb a few days before. It *hurt* poignantly that any face of such beauty should be

'ABDU'L-BAHÁ

so weary. We had brought letters from friends in America to give to him, but when we saw the weariness of his face, we could not bear to add at all to the burdens he has to carry.

And yet the weariness was not, I think, a weariness of spirit. I cannot tell why I felt that way—partly because he can reach, as no one else can, the infinite sources of spiritual strength.

I had no desire to speak to the Master; there was nothing that I could say. I do not know what happened in my mind and heart. There was no shock, no surprise, no sadness, no thought of my own faulty past. But I came to understand that for one who has been long in his presence, there can be no desire except to serve him; that one's life would be happy only as one pleased him; that one would be sad only as one grieved him. I felt then that I had begun to learn—that the will to serve was becoming greater, as I had prayed that it might. Having seen the Master but once, I could make no promise to myself that that longing would carry me through and beyond all my selfish habits of the past. But I knew that to be in his presence would mean that I must love him, that I must do his will.

After a time, perhaps half an hour, some English visitors came; the Master begged to be excused; we rose and watched him until he disappeared from sight. Afterward we walked about the garden at the front of the Tomb. We saw the big reservoir for rain water, built into the terrace, which supplies water for the garden and for many of the people of the neighborhood. Mírzá Luṭfu'lláh brought us figs from one of the trees in the garden. We looked across the beautiful blue waters of the bay, to 'Akká, shining in the distance. We caught a suggestion of luxuriant growth of trees, and were told that it marked the Tomb of Bahá'u'lláh. The sun sank behind the mountain, and finally Mrs. Hoagg said it was time for us to be going down, but that first we might see the interior of the Tomb.

The caretaker opened a door at the southwest corner of the Tomb, and spread a piece of matting in front of it. Mrs. Hoagg went with us to show us the custom used in entering the Tomb. We removed our shoes, and then the caretaker poured rosewater on our hands, from a little glass cruet. We followed Mrs. Hoagg into the first room. It was perhaps fifteen feet square, and the floor was covered with a beautiful dark Persian carpet. There was no furniture of any kind. Directly in line with the outer door was a second door that led into an inner room. That was also covered with beautiful rugs. Standing on the floor were exquisite glass vases with candles burning in them. They were in groups, perhaps of three, and they gave the impression of flowers of living flame. I think there must have been other objects, a few, in the room. But the whole impression was one of exquisite beauty, simplicity, and peace. The inner room was raised several inches above the outer, and the raised threshold was covered with an embroidered cloth.

Mrs. Hoagg walked slowly up to the threshold, knelt there a moment in prayer, and then came back to a corner of the room. Cora followed her, and then came my turn. I had heard of the custom of prostrating oneself at the threshold of the Tomb, and I had wondered whether it would not seem stilted and formal. But it did not in the least! Perhaps it was the dignity and majesty of the Tomb, perhaps it was because we had been with the Master so recently. I was filled with a feeling of humility, with a longing to be "evanescent at His threshold," and the kneeling in prayer seemed the most natural thing in the world! After that moment at the threshold, I walked to the back of the room while Sylvia and Mabel in turn went forward. We knelt in prayer a long time. I cannot guess what was in the hearts of the others, but my own was filled with a great longing to lose my old selfish self, and to acquire the unselfishness of service. It was a wonderful time. I thought of that "radiant youth called the Báb," who had given everything, friends, family, life itself, to prepare the way of the Lord. I thought of the Master and the years of imprisonment and hardship that he had spent in the service of the Blessed Beauty. For the first time since coming to Haifa, I was almost ready to weep—not from sorrow, but from the sense of the greatness of the power of God.

No thought of *death* entered my mind while I was there. It was not a place of *mourning!* When I thought of the Báb, it was to be happy that one so pure of heart had lived and served. The only grief was for my own faults and failures; and the *future*, with the hope of service, was much more vivid than the past!

Finally Mrs. Hoagg, Cora, and I had left the

Tomb. Mabel and Sylvia had not yet come out. We were about to put on our shoes, when suddenly the Master came around the corner! He smiled at us, and took up the cruet of rosewater. He held it out toward us, and I realized in a few moments that he wished to pour some on our hands. But I did not dream of going into the Tomb again, and so I did not realize what he meant! So he poured some on his own hands, put some on his face, and again held out the rosewater, giving us a glorious smile as he did so. That time we understood that he was waiting to anoint our hands, and we gladly held them out for the fragrant drops. Mrs. Hoagg whispered, "We will go in again"—and just then the men believers came in a long line from the front of the Tomb. The Master anointed the hands of each, and they passed into the Tomb. Each knelt at the inner threshold a moment, until all had risen, and stood in a circle about the room. Then the Master spoke to Rúhí Effendi, who began to chant a long prayer, one of the Prayers of Visitation.* His chanting was the sweetest, the most melodious

---

*See "Tablets of Visitation" in *Bahá'í Prayers* (Wilmette, Ill.: Bahá'í Publishing Trust, 1982) pp. 230–35. —ED.

of any I have ever heard. After the prayer the believers knelt at the threshold, and then passed quietly out. We four Americans were the last to leave, and as soon as we had left the Tomb, Mrs. Hoagg came to say that the Master was waiting to say good-bye to us. He stood at the northeast corner of the Tomb, and as we passed he shook hands with each of us, adding a caress for Sylvia. We turned and watched him as he walked back to the Tomb, waiting for the last glimpse! Then we walked down the mountain in the gathering dusk, and we were very happy. On the way down Mírzá Luṭfu'lláh told us interesting stories of the spread of the Cause in Persia, of the self-sacrifice and patience of the believers in trying to bring others to see the Light of this day.

Of the Master's talk on that first afternoon, I can remember the following: He said that we were very welcome, and inquired whether we were well. Then almost immediately he asked about Mr. Vail. Mrs. Paine said, "He sends his love and longing. He wishes to do the Master's will."

'ABDU'L-BAHÁ: "Mr. Vail is a good man, a sincere man. He is very illumined."

CORA GRAY: "It is through his teaching that we are here."

'ABDU'L-BAHÁ: "You must be very grateful to him. He has been the cause of your life. He has educated you. He has no aim save to serve the Kingdom.

"Some people are ready for education. They are like the fertile ground. Some have not capacity, they are like the barren or salty ground. His Holiness Christ has told a story of the seed that fell on stony ground and so it could not grow. Other seeds fell in the shallow earth, and they soon withered away. But some fell on the good fertile earth, and grew and produced fruit.* So it is with my words. Some fall on hearts that have no capacity; they do not take effect at all. Those people do not understand. Others hear and seem to understand, but they forget my words and do not live in accordance with them. But others have great capacity; they hear my words; they understand; they live accordingly.

"Have you seen Jináb-i Faḍl† in America?"

---

*Cf. Matt. 13:18–23 and Mk. 4:11–20.—ED.

†Mírzá Asadu'lláh Mázandarání, known as Jináb-i Faḍl, or as Faḍl-i Mázandarání.—ED.

CORA GRAY: "Yes, twice, just before we left New York."

'ABDU'L-BAHÁ: "He is a very pure-hearted man. He is a real Bahá'í. He is confirmed in service. He who is confirmed is confirmed in all things. Of the Persians who have gone to America only two have been fully confirmed Bahá'ís—his honor, Abú'l-Faḍl, and his honor, Faḍl. They are both very good."

Then the Master told the story of Mírzá Abú'l-Faḍl and the English ladies who insisted on seeing him! Finally, when they had knocked very persistently and continuously, Mírzá Abú'l-Faḍl became tired of hearing it, so he went to the door, and said, "Abú'l-Faḍl is not here." Up to this point in the story, the Master had been speaking in Persian or Arabic, and Rúhí Effendi had been interpreting, but when the Master came to this part, he spoke in English, very distinctly, and then repeated it, "Abú'l-Faḍl is not here!" and then he smiled the most adorable smile!

When we first saw the Master, he asked whether we had had any troubles or difficulties on the way. Cora replied that if we had had any, we had now forgotten all of them.

'ABDU'L-BAHÁ: "There is a Persian poet

who says that when one has attained to the goal of one's journey, the end of one's search, he forgets all that has happened on the way."

Cora said that the friends in Alexandria and Cairo had been so kind to us, and had helped us so much.

'ABDU'L-BAHÁ: "That is the duty of any Bahá'í. He is greater who serves most. That is the way to progress. Some flowers have color and no fragrance. Some have both fragrance and color; some have neither. So it is with the hearts of men."

SEPTEMBER 3, 1920. On September 3rd we did not see the Master at all, for he was still up on Mt. Carmel. I was very, very happy, with a calm peace. During the morning I wrote in my diary. In the afternoon, we had tea with the ladies at the Master's house. Someone told Mrs. Paine to sit in the big wicker chair at the end of the room, and she was happy to sit in the Master's chair. I talked to Ṭúbá Khánum for a time, mostly about education. Her daughter, Suraya, is to go to Cairo, to the Protestant School for Girls this year, and Ṭúbá Khánum was saying how much they disliked to have to send their children away from home. But the schools in Haifa are not advanced enough for study beyond the age of fourteen or fifteen. She said, "We like to have our children at home in the evening in order that we may give them some spiritual teaching ourselves." I could faintly imagine the loss to those children from separation from the lovely daughters of the Master! Ṭúbá Khánum said that the previous year Suraya had been in a girl's school in Beirut. She had been eager to go, for evidently life is a very restricted affair for a girl in Haifa! But this fall Suraya was not quite so eager to go to Cairo. Perhaps she had begun to realize how different her home in the Master's household is from the ordinary places of living!

We told the ladies that we hoped some of their children would come to America to study. But of course they think that a very long way from home to send them. Shoghi Effendi is now in England, just ready to enter Oxford, and Rúhangíz, his sister, is to enter some college for girls there.

Ṭúbá Khánum, and, on another day, Rúḥá Khánum, spoke of their hope of the founding of a Bahá'í School on Mt. Carmel. They are so sweetly appreciative and kind; they act as though the person to whom they are talking had all beautiful characteristics—and one longs to arise to meet that faith with deeds! Ṭúbá Khánum made me feel that way, when in speaking of a future Bahá'í school on Mt. Carmel, she said, "When such a school is founded I hope you may come and teach in it." What could be more wonderful! But one would have to "live the life" perfectly in order to be worthy to teach in such a school.

After a time Mrs. Paine told me to come over to sit in the wicker chair. That brought me near dear Rúḥá Khánum and the Holy Mother. They talked to me about education. The Holy Mother said that when I was teaching my classes I could show forth Bahá'í love and kindness, even though I could not directly give the Bahá'í teachings. Besides, she said, there were many of the Bahá'í teachings that I could mention in class, even though I did not label them "Bahá'í."

The Holy Mother is very, very sweet. She is quiet, calm, giving one the impression that no disturbance ever ruffles the evenness of her life. Her voice is low, and yet assured. There is a "sweet reasonableness" in it that seems to say, "Why be impatient? All will be well in God's good time!" She makes me think of the verse in the *Hidden Words*, "Be contented with what we have ordained for thy sake. This is for thy good if thou art content with it."* The Holy Mother *is* content with His will. She was not in the group of prisoners who were exiled to 'Akká in 1868, but came from Persia with her brother. The journey was very hard. Much of the time she had to sleep at night in the same room with several men, and therefore she had to wear a veil at night, as well as in the daytime.† Imagine the faith and courage of a young woman, who would come all that journey of months, through wild countries, in order that she might enter the Prison City, and marry —a Prisoner! When she reached 'Akká, the Bahá'ís had been removed from the barracks, and

---

*The Hidden Words, Arabic, No. 18. Shoghi Effendi's translation reads: ". . . be content with what We have ordained for thy sake, for this is that which profiteth thee, if therewith thou dost content thyself."—ED.

†Cf. *Munírih Khánum: Memoirs and Letters* (Los Angeles: Kalimát Press, 1986) pp. 26–44.—ED.

were living in a small house, one we saw when we visited 'Akká. One can only faintly imagine the warmth of the greeting she must have received when she came to be the wife of the beloved Greatest Branch! At that time the Master must have been twenty-seven or twenty-eight years old. We know that even then he was the comfort and joy of the whole Bahá'í colony!

One of the ladies apologized because they had not been over to the Pilgrim House to call on us, for they had been unusually busy. There is much to be done in that big household, and in addition, two or three of the children had been quite ill. I think it was Rúḥá Khánum who was saying that they wanted to see more of us, and she continued, "One should go and call on one's guests—and yet we do not!" Then she smiled and said, "But you are not our guests! You are members of our family!" What sweeter hospitality could one desire!

I have mentioned the big wicker chair at the end of the room. However, I never saw the Master sit in it! Whenever we saw him in that room, he sat in a corner on one of the divans—always in the same place.

I think it was this same afternoon that the ladies took us out and showed us the garden.

The whole plot of ground upon which the house stands is from one-third to one-half an acre in size, and all of it is a beautifully cared for garden, except for the parts where buildings actually stand. (There is nothing comparable in it to our American lawns of grass!)

The garden has all been made since 1911 or 1912, by one faithful Bahá'í who loves to serve the Master in that way. I think many of the seeds, cuttings, etc., have been sent by Bahá'ís from various parts of the world. The result of the gardener's work is a lovely place. Flowers, fruits, and vegetables of many varieties grow there. We saw peaches, lemons, and pomegranates hanging on the trees. The pomegranates were just ripening and one of the ladies picked some for us to taste. There were two varieties, a sweet kind, that everyone likes, and a rather sour kind which reminded us of our red currants. Cora and I liked its sharp tartness, but most of the others did not care for it. The pomegranates are a beautiful fruit, with their dozens and dozens of bright red drops, crowded together within the reddish-yellow rind.

The Greatest Holy Leaf walked about several of the garden paths, looking at all the plants and trees. Some one told us that that was the

'ABDU'L-BAHÁ IN THE GARDEN
of His house in Haifa.

first time in months that she had been in the garden! Apparently the ladies seldom go into the garden, because there are always men about who do not belong to the immediate family! And the Master says it is still not the time for the Bahá'í women in Haifa to go contrary to the custom of the country with regard to veiling when strange men are about. The ladies are longing for the time to come when they can lay aside the warm black veil!

To return to the garden: Several of the paths have trellises over them, with vines which make them very lovely. Above the main gateway there is a big bougainvillea plant which was covered with many blossoms when we were there. Beneath one of the arbors, against the house, and just below the Master's window, was a garden bench, where the friends often sat and talked. Cora and I went over there and sat for an hour two or three times, drinking in the beauty and peace. I had heard much of the Master's garden, and I was so happy to see it with my own eyes!

At dinner that Friday evening, the friends were very merry. There was a constant chatter, laughter, and teasing! Mírzá Badí' (who is interpreter for the English governor) sat next to Mrs. Hoagg, and they carried on a gay conversation. He has the nicest face, and his eyes twinkle with fun all the time!

We had watermelon for dessert. When the Master is not there to give the signal for leaving the table, it is the custom for all to watch until every one has finished eating; then all rise at once. But that evening, Malcolm and Mírzá Luṭfu'lláh lingered over their watermelon longer than the others!—I *think* Mrs. Hoagg and Mírzá Badí' were responsible for flashing a signal down the table that we should rise and leave them there! So some twenty-three people rose and looked on while Malcolm and Mírzá Luṭfu'lláh finished their watermelon, while everyone laughed at them! We were all like the simplest children who had played a prank on two playmates!

All day Friday we had been wondering when the Master would come down from the mountain. We were eager for him to come because we knew that we should see more of him then. And yet, remembering how tired he had looked, I could not help but wish he might stay longer in the quiet peace near the Tomb, in the hope that he might become more rested.

All that day I had been very happy and content not to see him, but as the evening came on I began to long to see his beautiful face again! And so I could not help but be happy when we heard that he was coming down the next morning—that Isfandíyár was to go up for him sometime between six and seven! And so I went to sleep in our quiet room in the Pilgrim House, rejoicing that on the morrow we should see him again.

SEPTEMBER 4, 1920. On Saturday morning, Cora and I rose in the darkness of 4:30 A.M., dressed, and by 5:15 we were on our way up the mountain toward the Tomb of the Báb. That early hour was a bit too late, for even then we found the climb warm, and the sun rose before we had reached the Tomb. We stopped to watch its glorious arising from behind the Lebanon hills. There were enough clouds to make a really beautiful sunrise. The valley of 'Akká was radiant, and the river winding through it gleamed silver! It looked, in its outward physical seeming, "a door of hope!" We continued up the hillside to the Tomb. As we passed the caretaker's house, he saw us, and by a gesture, asked whether we wished to enter his house. Perhap he thought we had come up to see the Master, whom we knew was either in the house or at the Tomb. But we motioned toward the Tomb. He smiled, and preceding us, opened the west door into the room where we had been on Thursday. Then he quietly departed.

The candles were not lighted and the central room was not quite so beautiful on that account. But a soft light filtered in through the doors—and the exquisite peace filled our hearts. We stayed for perhaps an hour, in meditation and prayer.

It must have been after seven when we went out into the garden. We walked about a bit, and then Rúhí Effendi and Mírzá Luṭfu'lláh came out to wish us good-morning. On the previous evening we had told Rúhí Effendi that we were going up to the Tomb early in the morning. But when he saw us there, he said, "You *really* came! I didn't think you would! Americans never get up early!" At which we laughed much! Rúhí Effendi's English is very good, but sometimes a phrase or some slang expression is used which he does not understand. He looks courteously questioning, half surprised, and waits for some one to explain!

The two young men talked to us for a few minutes, and then asked whether we would like to see the circle of cypress trees where Bahá'u'lláh used to sit. Of course we wanted to see them, and so Mírzá Luṭfu'lláh went with us, while Rúḥí Effendi went to the caretaker's house. I wondered whether the Master had already gone down the mountain, and decided that he probably had, because it was after seven.

Mírzá Luṭfu'lláh led us up a path, onto a terrace back of the Tomb, and there we saw the circle of cypress trees. There are ten of them, planted quite close together so that their boughs interlace, forming an almost solid wall. They are on a bit of ground which is raised about three feet from the surrounding field, and is held up by a stone wall. We went up into the circle of ground between the trees. Above our heads was a small circle of blue sky. The ground was brown with needles from the trees. I thought of the Blessed Beauty, and was glad that at one time in His storm-tossed life He had

THE GROVE OF CYPRESS
where Bahá'u'lláh rested.

been able to withdraw to that quiet green spot. But we had been there only a few minutes, when Rúhí Effendi came toward us, calling that the Master wished to see us! And we went on eager feet, following Rúhí Effendi to 'Abbás-Qulí's house.*

Cora was ahead of me, and she told me afterward that when she entered the room where the Master was sitting on a divan, she was not sure what to do! He bade her welcome, but still she stood in the doorway! Then he rose, held out his hands, and motioned her to a chair. She went and sat down. Just then I came in, and the Master motioned me to a chair beside Cora. I cannot remember whether he shook hands with us or not. (Usually he shook hands with us when we left him, but not when we came into his presence.) Mírzá Luṭfu'lláh and Rúhí Effendi sat by the door, and a tall Persian or Turkish man sat near us.

The room we were in had a north window, which looked out over the Bay of 'Akká. Like all windows in the eastern houses, it had several iron bars across it to keep out intruders. The house is high on the hillside, and there was

---

*'Abbás-Qulí is the caretaker of the Tomb of the Báb.—G.L.C.

a wonderful view across the bay. The Master sat on a divan in front of the window, and occasionally arranged some letters and other small objects, which he finally put into a small handbag. As he did this, he talked to us. He said, "This location here by the Tomb is very beautiful."

We said, "Yes, we enjoy it greatly."

Then he talked to us a little about the Báb. He said, "After the Báb was martyred, his body was kept in Persia for several years. It was never kept in the same place for more than a few years. Not many of the friends, even, knew where it was at any one time. After a long time it was brought here to Haifa, and placed in the Tomb on Mt. Carmel."

Cora asked how long ago it was brought here. I *think* the Master's reply was, about twenty-four or twenty-five years ago.

Cora asked Mírzá Luṭfu'lláh to say that we hoped that the Master was feeling more rested.

He replied, no, he was not rested, but that did not matter. And his expression implied that physical weariness was a matter of small concern.

'Abbás-Qulí brought to the Master a little tray with a teapot full of what looked like tea. The Master poured out some and drank it, explaining that it was a kind of herb drink. Then 'Abbás-Qulí brought us tea in the lovely little Persian glasses. Afterward, he came in with a tray full of things to eat and placed it on a chair in front of us. The Master told us to eat. "He says you must eat your breakfast here," Mírzá Luṭfu'lláh interpreted. We did not really want to eat—when we *could* be looking at the Master —but at his command we ate a little. The tray had on it ripe figs, ripe olives, honey, and slices of white bread—and the latter were the only slices of white bread we saw on our whole journey! I ate one or two figs, and a few olives. After a time the tray was passed to the tall Oriental next to us. Thus we had breakfast with the Master at the Tomb of the Báb! As we ate he was silent, looking out of the window upon the sea of 'Akká. His beautiful profile was outlined against the window; his gaze seemed to dwell on distant 'Akká—and I could not but think of those long years of imprisonment that he had spent in barred 'Akká. Some slight vision of all he had suffered swept over me. I knew then, beyond all question, that I had found him as the Master. My spirit knelt in humility at his feet.

After a while, he gave the bag he had been arranging to Rúhí Effendi, and said that he was ready to go down the mountain. We followed him from the house to where Isfandíyár was waiting with the carriage. We had expected to walk down the mountain, but after the Master had ascended to the middle seat, he motioned to us to get in the back seat. And so Cora and I rode down Mt. Carmel with the Lord of our hearts. No word was said, but we were very happy. At the gate of his house he alighted, and, saluting us with uplifted hand, he left us and entered his home!

At the Pilgrim House we found Rúhí Effendi and Mírzá Luṭfu'lláh, who had walked down and were there before us. Then we ate the breakfast that Fujita had prepared!

SEPTEMBER 5, 1920. This morning, all of us had finished breakfast at about 7:45 and were sitting at the table talking. No, Mírzá Muḥammad-Sa'íd had not finished; he had just come in, and was waiting for Fujita to bring him some tea. Suddenly, Mrs. Hoagg said, "The Master is coming!" She had seen him pass the window! We all rose, just as he entered the door. He came in like a ray of light and life. He

'ABDU'L-BAHÁ IN HAIFA
approaching the Pilgrim House in Haifa.
November 19, 1921.

sat down at the end of the table, bade us be seated; told Fujita to give Sa'íd Effendi his breakfast. But Sa'íd Effendi did not eat! He drank the tea Fujita brought, because, as he said later—that was not so hard to do, but he could not eat toast and eggs while the Master was speaking! We quite understood his feeling, as we remembered our experience at the Tomb yesterday morning!

The Master said that he hoped we were well and very happy. Then he asked again if we were well.

Mrs. Paine said, "We are all very well except Sylvia, who was a little ill in the night, but that is not serious."

'Abdu'l-Bahá replied: "I hope she will soon be well."

Sylvia smiled and nodded and the Master said, "That will soon pass away and you will be well again." Then he continued, "Your food and rooms are very simple here, but your purpose in coming here makes them seem good to you. When a man is *good*, all things about him are good. When a man is bad, all things about him are bad. It is necessary that man be very good."

After a pause the Master said, "You have

come here, and every day you try to improve. You try to improve more each day. You must become pure in heart. Then when you return to America, you must carry spirituality and inspiration with you. You must be like Jacob, who inhaled the fragrance of the garment of Joseph from a distance. But more than that, you must be one who carries the garment, who spreads the fragrances of the Spirit."

Turning to Mrs. Hoagg, the Master told her to take us to church this morning. Then he continued by saying, "The purpose of going to the church should be to worship. Turn your hearts to God and worship Him. One can worship God anywhere, in a church, in a mosque, in all places. But here I hope that you will go to the church."

Then he rose, smiled on us, said "Goodbye," and walked from the room, and down the steps. We went to the door, and watched him till he disappeared behind the wall.

I think that neither Cora nor myself had said a word all the time he was with us. I do not know how she felt, but for me, there simply was nothing that I could say. To be in his presence, to look on the beauty of his face, to listen to his voice, was all I wished to do. I do not know how or why, but in his presence, all life is *lifted* higher; it acquires freshness and beauty.

Mírzá Luṭfu'lláh translated the Master's words in this talk.

Following the Master's request we attended the little Episcopal chapel which is near the Pilgrim House. After our return from there, we called on Rúḥá Khánum for almost an hour, and such a happy time as we had! Her house is just next the Master's, so that she can easily help entertain the Master's guests, and yet look after her own household. She and her two sisters talked with us often, giving us wonderful stories about the Cause and instructing us in many ways. That day she told us about the Master's life, during the Great War;* how he gave food, money and encouragement to all those who sought his help, no matter what their race or religion. The people of the household lived on the simplest food in order that they might have food to share with the hundreds who came begging for bread. She told us, too, how few letters and papers came from the friends all over the world, and how they

*World War I.—ED.

longed for news of the welfare of the Bahá'ís in the different countries.

That afternoon after tea, we went over to the Master's house and talked with the ladies for a short time. Then word came that the carriage was ready to take us up the mountain, for the regular Sunday afternoon meeting. Ṭúbá Khánum, and one of her sons, Suhayl, went with us. In front of the Tomb many of the friends were gathered; more than forty, I think. For a time we talked with the people near us. Then Mírzá Luṭfu'lláh brought out the large guest book, and asked us to write in it our names, addresses, the date of our arrival in Haifa, and some word of greeting. Cora wrote, "The valley of Achor shall be unto them for a door of hope." Mrs. Paine wrote, "Beautiful beyond compare is Mount Carmel, the joy of the whole earth." And I added the sentence from the *Hidden Words* which I love so much, "Lift up thy heart with delight."* On that

---

*Probably, *The Hidden Words*, Arabic, No. 62. Shoghi Effendi's translation reads: "Lift up thy head from slumber, for the Sun hath risen to the zenith, haply it may shine upon thee with the light of beauty."—ED.

mountain one learns so much about *why* one should "lift up one's heart with delight."

In a short time the Master came from around the eastern corner of the Tomb, followed by little Fu'ád. The Master was radiantly beautiful. He wore a dove-colored overcoat or wrap, for the wind was cool on the mountainside. Fu'ád was dressed in a stiffly starched white dress, and made a staunch little bodyguard for the Master. (Someone told us that one night Fu'ád went up to the Master after supper and said, "You go to bed now and rest. I will take my gun and lie across the threshold. If any thieves come, I will scare them away!")

The Master gave us the talk about Elijah, which Mírzá Luṭfu'lláh took down in Persian, and later translated into English, so that we might have a copy of it. At the Tomb that day Mírzá Azízu'lláh interpreted for us.

As always the beauty of the Master's face, its power and majesty, held my attention so that it was difficult to listen to what he said. After the talk, the door at the west end of the Tomb was opened, and we all filed past the Master, who anointed our hands with rosewater. Never again will we be able to inhale that special rose fragrance, without the memory of that western entrance and the Master at the door, coming to our minds!

The candles were burning in the glass vases; there was utter stillness except when the Tablet was being chanted; and, as on the previous afternoon, my heart was won by the peace and glory of the place. While the tall, black-robed Bahá'í from 'Ishqábád chanted the prayer of Visitation in Persian, the Master stood in the doorway, and the room was filled with a divine radiance of Love. At the threshold of that Tomb one may lay all burdens down. Life becomes simple and straight because one feels surrounded with Divine Love.

After the meeting in the Tomb the carriage took us back down to the Pilgrim House, and then returned to bring the Master. Cora and I watched for his return for a long time, while the quick twilight faded into darkness. Soon above us, on the mountain, there shone out the light in front of the Tomb, which is lighted every night unless there is very brilliant moonlight. At last, the carriage drew up before the door of the Master's house, and we caught a glimpse of white as he swept down from the high seat, and we heard the murmur of his greeting to the men who were sitting in front of the gate, waiting for the call to go into dinner. So do all the pilgrims linger near his house, hoping that they may but glimpse his face as he passes by them.

That night at dinner, the Master said, "I hope the health of the friends is good. Today you went to visit the shrine (the Tomb of the Báb). Are you happy?" His smile, his care for our happiness and comfort, would have made anyone happy, and our smiles of reply must have been bright enough to show him a little of how happy we were!

For dessert that night we had grapes, although on every other night we had had watermelon. While we were eating the grapes, he said, "His Holiness Christ once was eating grapes. He said, 'I will not eat of the fruit of the vine again until I eat it with you in the Kingdom.'* But the grape of the Kingdom is other than these grapes. In the Kingdom there is no bread like this. Now also, I say to you all, we will eat together of the divine bounties, God willing, in the Kingdom—that is, divine food, heavenly food. Its taste is everlasting. Its sustenance is everlasting. God willing, there we all together will eat of that heavenly food."

*Cf. Matt. 26:29; Mk. 14:25; and, Lk. 22:18.—ED.

SEPTEMBER 6, 1920. On Sunday afternoon the Master said to us, "Tomorrow, I am sending you to 'Akká!" and his smile was light itself.

We left the Pilgrim House at about 8:00 A.M. Ḍíyá'iyyih Khánum, Mihrangíz, Riyáz, of the Master's household, and Isfandíyár, called for us. Mrs. Hoagg and we four people added five more to the group. With joy in our hearts we began the two hours' drive to 'Akká. Down through the narrow streets we rode, and then eastward past the railway station. We passed through a grove of tall palm trees, and down to the shore. At last! that beautiful "way of the sea," toward the Holy City, 'Akká! How often we had read of the journey along the white sand, where the horses' hoofs play in and out of the water, as they follow the hard-packed sand at the sea's very edge. We watched the waves rush up and then back, sweeping with them tiny sea animals. We passed trains of camels and donkeys, all on that universal highway "not made with hands."

We thought of all the happy, longing pilgrims who have gone to 'Akká that same "way." Doubly happy were we that our Master was living safely in his own house in Haifa, and not as a prisoner in 'Akká!

Always ahead of us was a glimpse of 'Akká, which shone more clearly as our three horses trotted along the shore. To the East, the hills of Lebanon were purple in the distance.

As we neared 'Akká, Mrs. Hoagg pointed out the walls, the gate, the cemetery where some of the Bahá'ís of that group of exiles are buried. Finally, Ḍíyá'iyyih <u>Kh</u>ánum pointed out the tower of the barracks.

Outside the gate we halted, for one of our horses had lost a shoe. The blacksmith was sitting under a tree, with his tools about him. But at Isfandíyár's request he came and put on the needed shoe. While we waited, we looked at the high wall of the city, which showed how much a prison city it had been. The walls were high and thick; the gate was small, and beyond the outer wall was a second inner wall. A long train of camels passed us, going into the city, and one tiny donkey, heavily loaded, came out! People in oriental garb drifted by us, and glanced at us curiously, but not in unfriendly fashion. I remembered the showers of stones from small boys with which the Bahá'í pilgrims to 'Akká used to be greeted, and I meditated on the changes that time brings!

We entered the gate, passed between the two walls for a distance, and on into the town. Isfandíyár stopped the horses at the foot of a long flight of steps. It was the way to the barracks. At the head of the stairway a soldier met us, and conducted us about, for the barracks are now occupied by a few soldiers. This man looked like an Arab, but he was under British orders, I think. He led us through many winding passages, showing us several places in which we had no special interest. But finally he led the way to the tower on the west side of the court, the tower where Bahá'u'lláh was imprisoned for two long years. Ḍíyá'iyyih Khánum told us of the various places associated with Bahá'í history. She showed us the room where Bahá'u'lláh had lived, the window from which He had looked out upon the plain of 'Akká. She showed us the rooms where the immediate family had lived, and the roof from which the Purest Branch* fell. The rooms were small,

---

*'Abdu'l-Bahá's younger brother Mírzá Mihdí, who fell to his death through a skylight in 1870, while imprisoned in 'Akká with his family.—ED.

THE "MOST GREAT PRISON" at 'Akká. The windows at the upper right, on the top floor, are those to Bahá'u'lláh's prison cell.

rude; a sad exchange for the royal palaces of Persia, as far as physical comfort was concerned. Yet joy was there, because they might suffer hardship in the service of God. To have been there in the days of Bahá'u'lláh—for that privilege one might have been able to bear much!

Afterwards we crossed the large court, and saw the pool, or reservoir, in the center, from which the exiles obtained the slimy water which was their only drink during the first twenty-four hours of their imprisonment! On the south side of the court we saw the rooms where most of the exiles were imprisoned. They are like rather wide and long corridors. At present they are quite well lighted, but Mrs. Hoagg said that the British have changed them a great deal, and have let in much more light. When she first saw them, they were very dark and gloomy. And in the days of the Turkish rule, they must have been very dirty, unwholesome, and dark. Here, amid all manner of privations and sufferings, the band of exiles praised God for having led them to believe in His greatest and newest Manifestation. As we walked about the barracks, Ḍíyá'iyyih Khánum told us stories of those early days, making them live again, for our instruction.

After we left the barracks, a few moments' drive brought us to another house* where the Bahá'ís had been imprisoned. Bahá'í families live in it now, and they welcomed us with sweet kindness. We saw the little room where Bahá'u'lláh lived for seven years. In an adjoining house, which now seems to be a part of the first house, the holy family lived for many years more. There Bahá'u'lláh's room has been left as it was when He used it. The windows overlook the sea; to the south there is a view of distant Haifa; to the north, the plain of 'Akká. I think Bahá'u'lláh practically never left the house while they lived there. We hear of 'Abdu'l-Bahá's caring for the physical needs of the friends, as well as it could be done under the very difficult conditions; engaging in trade that he might have money with which to equip a bath; in all ways constantly serving his father!

It was to the smaller of these two houses that the wife of 'Abdu'l-Bahá came from Persia. I am not sure, but I think that some of the daughters were born there.

In the family of Bahá'ís who care for these two houses, we met a woman, Sakínih Sulṭán,

*The House of 'Abbúd.—ED.

whose husband, at the age of twenty, was a martyr in Persia! When we were there she was probably over fifty years of age. A few years ago, her daughter died leaving a baby boy, Labíb, for whom she is now caring.

Whenever one is with these Bahá'ís who have been intimately associated with Bahá'u'lláh or 'Abdu'l-Bahá, one marvels at the spirit of service and self-sacrifice they show. We longed to acquire in its fullness that attitude of evanescent service.

It was after eleven when we left the city of 'Akká behind us, and drove toward the Riḍván. We went north of the city wall, toward the east. By strange track-like roads we drove, past gardens walled with cactus plants. It was perhaps a mile and a half or two miles before we came to the Garden—the Riḍván. Just before we reached it we turned to the south, and the road followed a little stream. We passed a water wheel, turned by a small donkey, and later we saw the water he had pumped, as it fell from a fountain in the garden.

At the gate we left the carriage, and Isfandíyár unharnessed the horses that they might have a well-earned rest.

How I had longed to see the Riḍván at

THE RIḌVÁN GARDEN in the Holy Land.

A WEEK IN 'ABDU'L-BAHÁ'S HOME

'Akká! That spot between "the two rivers," that garden on an island! It is a place of beauty and peace. Tall palm trees, pomegranate trees loaded with ripe fruit, beautiful vines bearing many-colored blossoms—all add to the beauty of the Riḍván. From the fountain, streams of water run to the north, south, east, and west, watering the plants.

But the place of most wonderful associations is the spot on the side of the stream, where the two great mulberry trees form the "tent not made with hands," "over land and water." There in the later days, the Blessed Beauty used to sit beneath the trees. It is a place of rest and peace. The troublous world seems very far away. Love and peace are in the wind, in the soft rustling of leaves, and the murmur of the water.

Our lunch was spread on a rug beneath one of the mulberry trees. We ate of the Persian foods from the Master's household, of the fruits from the Riḍván. We were utterly content to sit in that heavenly place and watch Riyáz, and another small boy who had come with us from 'Akká, sail boats down the tiny stream from the fountain.

THE RIDVÁN GARDEN

in the Holy Land. The planters mark the place where Bahá'u'lláh was accustomed to sit.

A WEEK IN 'ABDU'L-BAHÁ'S HOME

After lunch, we all rested for an hour or more, after which we had tea. It was too sweet a place to leave, but the hours were passing, and the supreme goal of our day was still ahead of us—the visit to the Tomb of Bahá'u'lláh. And so we left the Riḍván, with the prayer in our hearts that we might come again to that lovely garden of our Lord.

We drove to the north, across the rolling 'Akká plain, till the Bahjí appeared before us. Here Bahá'u'lláh lived after He left 'Akká, still technically a prisoner, but permitted to live among trees and flowers, instead of being shut in by the dark prison walls. At the Bahjí we turned westward, and soon rounded the corner of a long, low building, where the caretaker of the Tomb lives, Sayyid Abú'l-Qázim. There we alighted, and Ḍíyá'iyyih Khánum indicated a small gate into the garden. Slowly, with wonder in our hearts, we followed the path through the garden to the door of the Tomb. In the little outer room we removed our shoes. A short flight of steps brought us into the large room of the Tomb.

We found ourselves in a large room with a garden in the center. At the west end were several windows, and floods of light poured down

BAHÁ'U'LLÁH'S MANSION AT BAHJÍ
behind the Shrine of Bahá'u'lláh.

upon us from the glass windows in the roof. In the northwest corner of the room, a curtained door led into the Tomb itself.

Ḍíyá'iyyih Khánum drew aside the curtain, but the door was closed. We knelt in the space before the door, and Ḍíyá'iyyih Khánum chanted the Prayer of Visitation. I tried to remember the words of the Tablet of Bahá'u'lláh, "Cause me to drink of the cup of evanescence, clothe me in its mantle and immerse me in its sea,"* but my mind seemed almost a blank. I remembered the promise that the prayer one prays in all sincerity at the Tomb of Bahá'u'lláh shall be answered. With my whole heart I prayed for "evanescence" at His Threshold, and for the power to serve His Cause. Then I prayed for various people I knew, who were in need of a vision of the greatness of God's love. And then for the Bahá'í friends in America. . . .

And how I longed to enter that closed door, into the Tomb itself! I remembered that . . .

*Shoghi Effendi's translation reads: "Give me to drink from the chalice of selflessness; with its robe clothe me, and in its ocean immerse me." *Bahá'í Prayers* (1982), p. 235.—ED.

and . . . had been inside and that they had been somewhat surprised at being led in, for they knew that people were not always permitted to enter there. I realized how very far short I fell of the purity of heart of that party of pilgrims. I knew that the Master gives to each one what he most needs. And so it was as though the Master said to me, "You have not yet learned enough to appreciate the atmosphere of that inner room. Live the life; serve the Cause; achieve purity of heart. Then perhaps if you return here, the rewards of the pure in heart will be yours!" And with my whole mind and spirit I pledged myself to the accomplishment of that task.

We were in prayer at the threshold of the Holy Tomb of Bahá'u'lláh for a long time. Finally, Ḍíyá'iyyih Khánum went out toward the outer door. We followed her, ready to leave that place of light. But she returned, went to the front of the room, and opened the curtained door. I do not know why she did it; perhaps Mrs. Hoagg reminded her that it was our visit to the Tomb. But I am sure that in some way, the Master's will entered into it. When I fully accepted his will for me as my guide, "acquiesced," then my desire was granted.

THE SHRINE OF BAHÁ'U'LLÁH (center) with the Mansion at Bahjí behind.

The heavy curtains at some of the windows were pulled back, and the setting sun poured a radiant glory of light into the room. "His resting-place shall be glorious"—with torrents of physical light, as well as with spiritual glory. I do not know how long we knelt there. Time's passing ceased for us. My very breathing was a dedication of myself to our glorious leader, Bahá'u'lláh.

Our drive home was a silent one. I think we were all rather weary, physically, from our long day. But the spiritual significance of all we had seen filled us with so much to think about, that we had no desire for speech.

The sun set in the blue waters of the Mediterranean, in a majesty of color. Darkness came down and shut us in on that crescent sea shore. The horses sped along through the darkness, toward the distant lights of Haifa. We were eager to be again in the Master's presence.

We reached Haifa a short time before the dinner hour, weary, but happy. At dinner that evening the Master said, "Did you have a happy day in 'Akká?" And we replied, "Oh, yes, it is a day we shall always remember!"

He replied, "You *must* always remember it! It must be like images cut in tablets of stone!"

That evening as he bade us good-night, after

'ABDU'L-BAHÁ IN THE GARDEN
near the Shrine of Bahá'u'lláh.

dinner, he said in his dear, measured English, "Go—and rest! Go—and rest!"

By the Master's love for us, we know something of the love of Bahá'u'lláh. And from the love of Bahá'u'lláh we know of the Love of the Infinite Father, whose voice comes to us through the Supreme Pen: "I knew My Love in thee, therefore I created thee; upon thee I laid My Image, and to thee revealed My Beauty." "I loved thy creation, therefore I created thee. Wherefore love Me that I may acknowledge thee and in the Spirit of Life confirm thee."*

SEPTEMBER 8, 1920. On the morning of September 8th, I went alone to the Tomb of the Báb at sunrise. Cora had not been sleeping well, and so she did not feel like rising at 4:30

The Hidden Words, Arabic, Nos. 3 and 4. Shoghi Effendi's translations read: ". . . I knew My love for thee; therefore I created thee, have engraved on thee Mine image and revealed to thee My beauty" and "I loved thy creation, hence I created thee. Wherefore, do thou love Me, that I may name thy name and fill thy soul with the spirit of life."—ED.

that day. But I woke, dressed and was almost to the Tomb before the sun rose. When his full splendor began to loom above the horizon, I sat down on a stone in the field below the *musáfir-khánih* (Pilgrim's House), and watched the lord of day cast his first light across the valley of 'Akká.

After a time I went on up to the Tomb, passing along the path with its beautiful cypress trees. At the Tomb I entered the room on the east side and stayed there in prayer and meditation for almost an hour. The tall Bahá'í from 'Ishqábád came in and knelt in prayer for some time, and then chanted. After he had gone, a younger man whom I did not know came in and chanted very softly and sweetly. He went out and I was alone for some time. The folds of the long veil I wore fell about my face and shoulders, and seemed to shut me in with God. His radiant Presence was very near.

I tried to fill my heart with the exquisite beauty and peace of that heavenly place, for I knew that was my last morning on the mountain. I knew that many and many would be the times that I would long to be kneeling at that Threshold.

Finally, I knew that it was time to be going

down the mountain. Just as I was leaving the Tomb, Mírzá Luṭfu'lláh came in. I went out into the garden, and walked about a bit, drinking in the beauty of flowers, hills, water, and sky. Soon Mírzá Luṭfu'lláh came out and bade me good-morning. Then he suggested that we gather jasmine blossoms to take down to the Pilgrim House. So we pulled off dozens of the fragrant flowers, and filled our pockets and handkerchiefs with them. Later we strewed them on the breakfast table. Mírzá Luṭfu'lláh said that he used to fill a basket full of blossoms, stripping the bushes each morning. He took the basket to the Master, who scattered them everywhere he went.

About 7:00 A.M., we started down the mountain. Mírzá Luṭfu'lláh had a stone bruise on his heel, and was wearing a loose slipper and carrying a cane; but never once did I hear him complain about it. Instead, he talked of how the Master works with no thought of physical fatigue. He works all day long, interviewing callers, etc. He goes to bed possibly by 9:00 or 9:30, but often he is up again at midnight, chanting and praying. Then he may correct Tablets for a while, and then sleep two or three hours more. And at perhaps 6:00 A.M. he rises for the day's work! Apparently, he averages not more than four to six hours of sleep a night! So his whole life is given to the service of mankind.

Mírzá Luṭfu'lláh said, "The real Bahá'í activity is not to stay here in the light of the Master's love. It is to go out into the world and spread his message of service. Be happy that you are going out to work for him."

But at another time he said, "Pray for us who live here in the Master's household. We have many temptations to guard against. We must never become impatient or give way to any depression. Not long ago when the Master was speaking to us, he said, 'You must be an example to all who come here. In you they must see what a real Bahá'í should be.' So we need your prayers that we may live up to that work."

We had thought of the great joy of being a member of the Master's family, but then we began to realize that only those of great unselfishness may be his helpers there in Haifa.

On that beautiful morning, we entered the Pilgrim House before breakfast was quite ready, and strewed the jasmine blossoms over the table.

The Master came in after breakfast, and stayed only a few minutes. He smiled at us all, and we were very happy to be near him. He asked especially about Mrs. George's health. He said a few words to her, smiled at all of us, and then rose and left us. We all went to the door and watched him as he disappeared through our gate.

After breakfast, we went over into the Master's garden, and waited for an opportunity to talk with him for a few moments. After a while Rúḥá Khánum called Mabel and Sylvia in to see him. While they were gone we stood talking with Mrs. Hoagg and some of the young men. I shall not forget the look on Mrs. Hoagg's face when she spoke of the Master's longing for unity among the friends. His only happiness is to know of the increase of unity among the believers, and of their spreading the Cause. His face always becomes sad if he hears of any contention or lack of harmony. "If people in America could see the Master, could realize how he works, they would never do anything to sadden him," she said. When one is in the Master's presence it seems utterly impossible that one should ever do anything that would sadden, or make any heavier the load of work he carries! "In the light of his holy presence, all desire dies save the desire to be like him."

'ABDU'L-BAHÁ
on the steps of His house in Haifa.

Later in the morning, Cora and I were called in to see the Master. Rúḥá Khánum translated for us. We gave the Master the letters we had brought from American friends. We asked him to bless the ringstones and rosaries we had bought at Mírzá Inayatu'lláh's shop. He took them in his hands, said a few words that must have been a prayer, kissed them, and handed them back to us. And so we brought back to America Bahá'í ringstones made doubly precious by his touch of love.

The Master said that he was sorry not to have seen us more, but that he had been very busy while we were there. "But," he continued, "it is not the length of time that one spends here that is important. Some people stay a short time, and then go and do great service. Other people are here a long time, and they learn nothing. There is some wood that is very dry: it catches fire quickly and burns well. There is other wood that is so wet that it will not burn even though you should try for a whole day. There is no result but smoke. It will not blaze, it will not keep any one warm; it will not even cook anything!" As he said the latter he smiled. But when Rúḥá Khánum translated it, Cora laughed out loud. That seemed to delight the Master, for he laughed very heartily with the most unaffected enjoyment.

Cora asked how one should teach the Bahá'í Movement to our United States southerners, among whom race prejudice is so strong. He said, "Go slowly at first. Be kind and courageous and patient. Live the Bahá'í life among these people. Do not mind if they oppose you. Their prejudice is so strong. It is like a religion. But when they become Bahá'ís they will be very good and sincere ones. But at first teach the principles and be kind to them. The rest will follow in time."

After this, we went and talked with some of the ladies of the household. Soon the Master called for Mabel and Sylvia, and gave Sylvia a Bahá'í name, Badí'iyyih, which means "something new and wonderful." We were not present when he gave her the name, but Mabel said that he walked up and down the room, radiating power and love.

When Sylvia came back with her new name, the Holy Mother brought out a box of candy, in honor of Sylvia's nameday. The candy was white with a little chocolate center. Bringing it out in Sylvia's honor was one of the sweetest, kindest acts of simple thoughtfulness that we saw in Haifa. Needless to say, Sylvia Badí'iyyih Paine was a very happy girl that day.

It was on that morning that the Greatest Holy Leaf showed us the pictures of Bahá'u'lláh and the Báb. We had already seen pictures of the Báb, and so I think most of our attention was centered on the photograph of Bahá'u'lláh. The pictured face was of dignity, power and majesty. But the feeling of the power, the glory, the supreme Reality of Bahá'u'lláh which came to me in Haifa, did not come from seeing His photograph. That Reality is living and vibrant in the unselfish lives of the friends; it makes radiant the atmosphere of the Tomb on Mt. Carmel and the Tomb at Bahjí; it shines from the Master's eyes.

Later in the morning, Cora and I were sitting on a bench in the garden, just below the window of the Master's writing room. Occasionally his voice floated down to us, as he dictated or talked with a caller. Once he came out of the house, and walked to the corner of the garden, where some masonry was being done. Soon he returned, and his voice was again heard from his room. Such brief glimpses made us very happy, for he radiates such life that one is lifted toward supreme joy just to know he is near. In his Essense he is so detached from earthly things, he is so different from all human beings one has ever seen, he is Love incarnate.

Mírzá Azízu'lláh came and talked with us for a while, and told us stories about the European Bahá'ís whom he had visited not long ago. Other friends passed and stopped for a word. It was a perfect morning and we were sorry when the lunch hour called us back to the Pilgrim House.

After dinner that evening, Rúḥá Khánum took us to receive the Master's farewell. I can remember very little of what he said. He told us that his love and thoughts and prayers would go with us. He sent his love and greetings to all the Bahá'ís in America.

I knew that I should not see him again, but I felt no sadness or grief. His love was too great: it poured in a radiant flood about me, and held me suspended in a priceless moment, when time stood still, and I lived in eternity. His eyes were glorious stars of light and love. No words can express their beauty.

He shook hands with us in parting. When he said good-bye to Sylvia, he smiled down at her and said, "Sylvia!—Badí'iyyih <u>Kh</u>ánum!—*Miss* Badí'iyyih!"—and his voice was filled with the most affectionate and sweet laughter!

Thus we left the Master's house, that wonderful home, of which he has said, "My home is the home of peace. My home is the home of joy and delight. My home is the home of laughter and exultation. Whoever enters through the portals of this home must go out with gladsome heart."

Next morning, before daybreak, we ate our last meal in the Pilgrim House and said farewell to our happy housemates there. Sa'íd Effendi, Mírzá Luṭfu'lláh, Rúḥí Effendi, and faithful Isfandíyár and his horses, took us to the train which left at 6:00 A.M. We had a half-hour's talk with the young men before the train pulled out—but of that time I remember clearly one thing. Mírzá Luṭfu'lláh turned to us as he said good-bye, and added, "Be good! Be good!" Then he smiled and said, "You know what I mean!" And no one who had seen the members of the Master's household for a week could fail to know that "to be good" is love and service and the spreading of the ideals that the Master teaches.

'ABDU'L-BAHÁ
walking in the streets of Haifa.

In the *Hidden Words* Bahá'u'lláh has said, "If thou run with all immensity and speed through the space of heaven, thou shalt find no rest save in obedience to Our Command and in devotion before Our Face."* In Haifa one learns, as never before, the meaning of that sentence. The will to obey, a longing for devotion, are born in one's heart and spirit.

Since we left the Master's home, the days and weeks and months fly past, and are filled with many duties; many calls to help in the work of the world. But the beauty of the Master's face is with us. "In the light of His Holy Presence all desires die save the desire to be like Him."

Alláh-u Abhá!

---

*The Hidden Words, Arabic, No. 40. Shoghi Effendi's translation reads: "Wert thou to speed through the immensity of space and traverse the expanse of heaven, yet thou wouldst find no rest save in submission to Our command and humbleness before Our Face."—ED.